ONCE IN A LIFETIME

By

Lawrence Pfaffendorf

ISBN: 1-4107-2040-3 (e-book)
ISBN: 1-4107-2041-1 (Paperback)
ISBN: 1-4107-3944-9 (Dust Jacket)

Library of Congress Control Number:
2003091493

This book is printed on acid free paper.

Printed in the United States of America
Bloomington, IN

1stBooks - rev. 4/18/03

Acknowledgement page

Once In A Lifetime is a book about my life as I remembered it.

THANKS TO:

My mother and father, William Frederick Pfaffendorf and Anna Catherine Thompson for being my parents.

To my granddaughter Katelyn Arquette for helping to make this book possible.

To my daughter Pamela for her understanding and editing.

To my wife Elaine and my family for their help.

I was born against great odds as everyone is, and I wish to share the fun, sadness, and hope my life has been, and to leave a note that Larry was here.

I was born in Georgetown, northwest of Kennan, Wisconsin on April 9, 1934. My parents were William Frederick Pfaffendorf and Anna Catherine Thompson. I had two older sisters and one younger brother. Our family was very spread out. The oldest girl Adelaide Margaret, was born September 1, 1920 in St. Paul, Minnesota. Emma Bernice, was born April 19, 1926 in Kennan,

Wisconsin. I, Lawrence William, was born April 9, 1934. Then finally, Garey Bruce, born April 2, 1937. When I was born, my father was 45 years old and my mother was 34. They were tired from work and age, so us boys were not supervised as well as the girls. My parents' children were born with seventeen years between the oldest and the youngest. They had children in school from 1926 to 1955, a total of 29 years with only four children.

Well, let's go back to where my life began. It was Sunday, April 8, 1934, about five o'clock in the evening, when mother got her

In back row left to right: Garey, Larry

In front row left to right: Bernice, Dad, Mom,

Adelaide

Anna Thompson and William Pfaffendorf's wedding, October 8, 1919. My Mother and Father.

first labor pain. She had just finished up the evening chores with Dad and was starting for the house, the lantern showing her way as she came up the path.

The smell of the barn and hay was still fresh on her clothes. As she looked ahead, she saw the lamp in the house where their little girl was playing while she had helped milk cows.

The smoke from the chimney drifted across the almost full moon. She looked to the north of the house and saw the two spruce trees that Dad had planted when their two girls had been born. Adelaide in 1920 and Emma or Bernice as we called her by her middle name, in 1926. That's when the pain hit, and she stopped to rest. As she looked again at the two trees, she thought, "Willie, you are going to have to plant another tree this spring."

Willie was what she always called my dad. She made it to the house and Bernice came running to see her. In a moment, my dad came in too. Mother said, "Willie, it's time for the baby."

So my dad went out and hitched up the team. There were no cars or telephones. No one had a phone on our road. It must've taken quite a while for him to harness the two horses by only lantern light.

I can imagine that as my dad drove briskly along, he thought about this third child to be born, and how his life was changing so fast. He had the two girls already. Adelaide was away in Kennan going to high school, and the other one was Bernice.

My dad had been in World War One and wanted to forget about it. He said he wanted to have peace and quiet, so he came to this dead end road in northern Wisconsin, six miles northwest from Kennan, bringing along his wife and daughter Adelaide.

He hurried the horses to a faster pace so he could get back before Annie had this child.

He had spent the day fighting forest fires close by, so he must have been very tired. He brought Mrs. Larson to our little house of one big room, a basement, and an upstairs. No insulation anywhere, just bare 2x4's, no wall board. The electric came in 1946. Then we had lights, but never a telephone. Dad also had to take Bernice to Grandpa Thompson's place, a half a mile to the north.

Mrs. Larson told years later about sitting with my mother all night half asleep. The wood stove made shadows on the wall as it burned to keep the house warm. The kerosene lamp was turned down low, and Dad was upstairs sleeping. As the night wore slowly on, between labor pains, they listened to the wolves howl in the Million Acre Swamp, and an owl in the big

Basswood tree that hooted as they waited for me.

As dawn broke quietly and a beautiful sunrise began, I came hollering and crying into this world. So much for Dad's peace and quiet. Those days were gone. In those days, there were no painkillers or pills to help the mother like there is today.

Mrs. Larson had a baby boy that was about two weeks old with her. She breast fed him and cared for him, and along with caring for my mother and I, she also made breakfast for my dad.

After breakfast, my dad went over to Grandpa Thompson's to bring Bernice home. My dad loved to play jokes, so he told Bernice that he had a surprise for her at home. She thought it must be a new calf, but when she came in the door and saw the Larson baby, she said, "We have a new baby, and he's so cute!" Mrs. Larson said, "No Bernice, that's my baby. Yours is over by your mother." She ran over and with astonishment in her eyes, she said,

"This one is cuter anyway." I think that was the last nice thing she ever said about me.

She was eight years old. She had been Dad's girl, and the only child at home. Boy, she sure had it made until I came along.

A boy had been just what my dad had wanted. The neighbor Lyle Cronk said my dad couldn't button his shirt for two weeks, because his chest was so popped out with pride that he had a son to carry on his name.

Oh yes, a name. That's what this boy needs.

Several days went by, and Dad walked down to

Alvin Sitan's place about three miles away and

called the doctor in Prentice to come check us

out. His name was George McKinnon. He was

a Scotsman and he knew the value of money,

so he lifted me and said, "Willie, you have a

twelve pound son." I don't think I weighed

twelve pounds until I was three years old, but

he knew that fathers wanted a big strapping

son, then they would pay him more for his call.

Dad paid him five dollars. That was during the

Great Depression, and Franklin Roosevelt had

been in office for only one year, so five dollars

was a lot when men worked for a dollar a day. If they were lucky.

Then the doctor said, "What name should we put on his Birth Certificate?" I don't know if they had talked about it before, but Mother said, "Lawrence William Pfaffendorf."

Here I am, one week old and trying to survive the smoke from the forest fires and they hang a name like that on me. Worst yet, Lawrence Grant had been my mother's boyfriend before she married Dad. Then William after my dad. He got second billing.

Dad always called me Lawrence never Willie or Billie. Thank goodness for that.

Then came time for baptism. We traveled to Kennan Lutheran Church about six miles away. I don't know how we got there, we had no car. I was baptized in the only clothes I had. Some underwear and wrapped in a blanket, no frills.

Ray Hampton and Margaret Sitan were my godparents. Margaret was Alvin Sitan's wife and Ray Hampton lived with them. In later years, I found out that Margaret and Ray were lovers. So my first years were hard on me.

First, I took my sister Bernice's place with our dad. Boy, I hate to think what happened when she baby-sat with me. Then named after mother's old boyfriend, and last, my godparents were lovers. WOW! What did I get into? I don't of course remember any of this, but it was told to me by my dad, mother, and others.

left to right: Ray Hampton, Elmer Johnson, Elvera Johnson [Elmer's sister], Betti Lou in Bernice's arms, Margaret Johnson, Margaret Sitan, Garey and Larry in front of Ray's old Buick and our house.

My dad and mother were good to me as I grew older. Mother would read to me and tuck me in, and Dad would sometimes play the violin and sing. They were always home for me, while nowadays, everyone works out someplace. The sounds at night around our happy little home were so nice, and the stars were so bright as the moon passed slowly over our happy little home. I was born into a farm family, hard working, honest people, who worked to clear the land to farm and feed their family. My father's family farmed, and so did my mother's.

My dad was born on St. Patrick's day and my mother was born on April Fool's day. My dad's parents lived in Minnesota. They were Herman and Emma Pfaffendorf. Grandma Pfaffendorf died the next year in 1935. Dad married Mother in 1919. Her name was Anna Catherine Thompson. Her mother had died when she was born. I would believe she was thinking of this as she waited for me to be born. Her mother died April 9, 1900. Exactly thirty four years later, I was born. Life is full of surprises.

My brother Garey arrived three years later on a dark and cloudy day. I asked my dad, "Where did he come from?" He said, "Mrs. Larson found him in the cabbage patch." I said, "Tell her to stay out of our cabbage patch. We don't need no more babies like him." It must've worked, because he was the fourth and last child.

My life as a child was a busy time. I, like everyone else, learned basic things, like who was in charge. Dad ran the farm and all the outside things. Mother handled discipline and the house, and taught us to write and read. As I was born left- handed, Mother tried the best she could. When I started school, they tried to help me, but they only way they could help me was right- handed. They had twenty- five other kids, so they didn't spend any extra time on me. So now, I can't write well with either hand!

A little about the Fairview school, some books say Farview school, that's not right. The road that runs from Highway 8 north two miles is called Fairview, because it goes by the Fairview School. Woodshed was what people called the first schoolhouse, built in 1923. Seventeen children and one teacher, Christina

Johnson. In 1932 and 1933 they built a new school. That was the one I attended.

I started first grade in the fall of 1940. no bus, no Pre- school, and no physical education. We got our physical education every morning and night when we walked a mile through the scary woods to and from the Fairview school. It had one room, one teacher, and twenty-six kids.

When I started at school, there were four kids in the first grade. Me, Marlyss Hvass, Lester Heacock and Donna Lee Cronk.

Larry and Garey in 1940

Marlyss Hvass' dad was the teacher. Clifford Hvass. He had all eight grades and twenty-six kids. That included the Ryders, Larsons, Hvasses, Heacocks, Cronks, Figuras, Sokolowskis, the Darotas, and of course, the Pfaffendorf family. Later, the Peaovers, Thompsons, Banyais, Barbeaus, Greenwalts, Timmers, and the Perdums families came.

Mr. Hvass was a great teacher. He always came and played ball with us at noon. Only, we played differently than you do today. We had our own rules. It was called Work-Up. You started out in left field, then go to right field, shortstop, pitcher, catcher, and then to batter. We didn't have any basemen or gloves! You would be out if someone caught your fly. Or if you were running bases, they could throw it at you. If the ball touched you, you were out. And, oh the big boys liked to throw it so hard at the little kids. When it hurt so bad you couldn't stand it, you stood by the schoolhouse and cried until you were ready to go back to playing. The longer it took you, the more kids got ahead of you, so back to left field you went.

In later years, we went to other schools. We learned how to play ball and even got gloves. Both boys and girls played ball, there were no sissies. One time, the school board brought us a basketball! We didn't know what that was until we started high school. We were slow learners.

We had four swings. Boys with guts would swing up and over the top pole. I never had a desire to do that. There was also a thing called Giant's Strides. It was a big steel pole in the middle with a dozen chains hanging down with three handles on them, so you could run around as fast as you could. Of course, the girls and little kids always let go first. Then the chains would come back around and hit you on the head or someplace. That felt so good. One time, before I went to school, my sister Bernice was playing on it and fell off and broke her collar bone. They took her to Dr. Francis in Kennan, and he fixed her up the best he could.

I was sick a lot when I was a kid. One time I was in bed for two weeks. I couldn't walk, so Bernice and my brother Garey each took a side and helped me walk again. What I had, who knows, I never went to the doctor.

Bernice got the measles one time, on the last week of school. How could she do that to us?! They had to call Dr. McKinnon to see her, and he said, "Oh, she'll live. That'll be fifteen dollars." Because of her, we couldn't go to the last day of school. We had waited all year for it too.

There were all sorts of food that we normally wouldn't get during the year, like ice cream. We did have ice cream occasionally when Mother's brother John came with his ice cream churner. It was so worn out that they had to put two dimes in the bottom by the shaft to keep it working. Then we took turns turning the handle. Boy, was that good! We had ice cream every year at the picnic except during World War Two. Then we had Sherbert. Yuck. That was not good. Every mother and grandmother brought a special dish for dinner. The men played ball with the kids. The older men would play horseshoes. That was new to us. The women would also talk about things and watch the little kids play. We also got our report cards, to see if we went on to the next grade…or not.

In 1946, Mrs. Helen Barbeau was the teacher, and Joe Figura was in the eighth grade. He had helped her all year, carrying wood from the woodshed, bringing in water from the pump out front to fill the red wing crock that held our drinking water, and all of her other dirty jobs. Yes, you guessed it, she failed him. They don't know why. Probably because she was having a lot of trouble at home at that time.

Christmas was always a wonderful time. We didn't get much for gifts, but no one did. Every kid had a part in the school play, and we worked hard to memorize our parts, so our parents would be proud of us. My dad was always full of jokes. One Christmas, Bernice wanted a nail polish kit, so Dad found an old one someplace, wrapped it up for her and put it under the tree at school. Wow! When she opened it in front of all the other kids, was she mad! One other time, he wrapped up a rutabaga for her and put it under the tree at school. She didn't like that either! She was so hard to buy for.

One Christmas, Bernice was sick with appendicitis and had an operation at

Ladysmith, and Mother stayed with her. So came the night of the Christmas play. Mother's brother, Andrew, who stayed with us sometimes, had to dress us. I remember he cut down one of his shirts for me, and that's the way we went. If Adelaide didn't send us pants and things, I don't know what we would've done. Not much money for Christmas that year. Mother and Dad bought a Webster's Dictionary from the Jewel Tea man, who came once a month to our house. They hid it in a big trunk upstairs. But, as kids are kids, I found it and then knew what I had coming on Christmas day. When Christmas day came, I had to look surprised. That's all I got that year. I never looked again, it spoiled my Christmas.

Dad had to sell two cows to pay for Bernice's operation, so it was not a good year. Now that it was war time, they had books and stamps for gas, sugar, flour, and tires. If you had the stamps, you maybe didn't have the money. The school collected all the metal junk for the war effort. We bought savings bonds and savings stamps. We also picked milkweed pods for life jackets for the army. Almost everyone had someone in the service. Some families had gold stars in their windows. It meant that their son had died fighting. Our family had Andrew in the service. Andrew was Mother's oldest brother, and he was some guy. He would buy anything and try it. He bought an old, yellow Willis Night car. A 1938 model. It didn't run long, so he parked it by the horse barn and it stayed there until he died. He bought rings and valves to fix it, but he never did. Us boys drove it a million miles and never left the farm. He told us to stay away from it. That lasted about a day, and we were back driving it again. He bought kits to make paper flowers, and when he got tired of that deal, we helped our little hands to it, and for many years we played with that stuff. He bought a zither to play from a traveling salesman, but he never used it. Us kids played with it that's all. One time, he bought several swarms of bees, and put them across the road to the east on wild land no one lived on. Well, a bear got into them, so he set a trap. The next morning, I was about six years old, Dad took me over to see it. The bear was, of course, mad. He lunged at us and came about two inches away. Wow, that was close! When I told my mother about that, she gave my dad some advice about it. You can imagine what it was! Bears were very rare back then, so people came all day long to see it. They came from all over. Finally, they shot it, and John and Andrew took it all over Kennan and Hawkins to show it.

One time at Fairview school, about fourth grade, I didn't do my spelling work, and the teacher, Mrs. Halverson, told me to stay after school. Being the wise guy that I was, I snuck out with the other kids and made it as far as the mailboxes. Then she called, "Lawrence! Get back here now!" The schoolbus was there picking up the kids and everyone knew I had to go back to do my work. Of course, I was crying. As I went by the schoolbus, Marlyss

Hvass was there and said, "Don't cry Lawrence. That was so nice of her." I never thanked her for that. Thanks.

One thing we did for fun at school was build brush houses out in the woods to the west of the school. Also to the north if too many kids were in one area. Me and Marlyss Hvass always played, and we had little kids for family. Marlyss and I went to school together for eleven years. I only missed the eighth grade, because I went to the Four Corners School. Anyways, when we built these houses, we all had to help each other, and we all had to bring a tool. I took a crate hammer, it had a hatchet, a nail puller, and a hammer all in one. I kinda forgot to ask my dad if I could take it, so I had to bring it home every night. Like he wasn't going to use it during the day and just at night. No way. One day, it got out of my school bag somehow, and as luck would have it, my dad came home after us at his fifteen mile per hour speed, and found the hammer. He came in the house and said, "Annie, look! Now I have two hammers alike!" We knew better. He went to put it in the tool shed and his was gone! He put two and two together real fast. He was pretty hot for a while. Then he got over it, and we had a lot of laughs about Dad's extra hammer. I bought myself one now, from a sale, and laugh about it whenever I look at it.

In the summertime, we played outside all day and did lots of stuff. We made go-carts to push. We had old wagon wheels. We stapled them on a board, one pair, that was stapled pretty tight, and the front had only one staple in the middle so we could turn it. Pretty smart wasn't it? One time, my sister Adelaide came home for a week's vacation which she did every year. This time, I remember she came with her two daughters, Margaret and Bettie-

Lou. Us boys were playing down by the horse barn, and she came with the two girls and said, "You guys can watch these girls for a while." We didn't like that at all. We had more important things to do. I told the girls that, and I looked around and there was Adelaide. She heard me. She gave me a good sermon, and I never forgot that.

We had a push lawn mower to mow our lawn, so one day when things were slow, Garey and I thought that it would run real good. So I told Garey to jump on. I always let him try things first. He jumped on and as I pulled the mower, the blades came around and cut his butt. He got a little behind in his play that day! I was always nice to my brother. I let him go first in anything we did.

One Sunday morning, we got ready for church in all white shirts and suit pants. As we waited for Mom and Dad to dress, we walked outside. I spied the young calves in the lane. I said to my brother, "I bet you could ride them, you're a pretty big kid." So we caught one and put Garey on it's back. Then I untied the calf and they were gone down the lane. When they came to the end of the lane, the calf stopped. Garey didn't. He wasn't as good a rider as I thought he was. Off he went, right into a nice fresh cow pie. Oh, are we in trouble! "What do you mean, we?" I asked Mother. "I tried to tell him he couldn't ride those calves, but you know Garey." He was crying to hard to say anything and she wasn't too happy too have to clean up that kid again. I told him, he should have known better.

Another time, we were playing cowboys and Indians with our brand new Red Riders BB guns. We went our separate ways, Garey to the barn, and I to the house. I went around the house, down into the basement, and upstairs where we had an open dormer window. So I waited. Soon Garey came sneaking up from the barn to the woodpile, he popped up for a look around. I raised my trusty Red Rider and hit him right between the eyes. Wow, he ran for the barn. I let him have two more shots. What was I supposed to do? I couldn't let that darn Indian in the house. I guess I won that round.

It might seem like we were always in trouble, but some days, in the summer, we were nice kids. One of those days, we had a windstorm, and it blew a nest of sparrows down, so we decided to help them. There was a wren house a couple of steps away, so we opened up the top, and in they went to their

Jip and Garey

new home. As you might know, there's a little difference in size there. The wrens accepted them and worked day and night to feed them. You can bet on the way south that fall they must've told their friends, "You should've seen the size of those two kids of ours!"

Mrs. Larson's place was always a good place to go. Lots of kids to play with and goodies to eat. One day, she had fresh raisin bread. I had never seen that! So I was picking the raisins out, and Mother said, "What are you doing?" And I said, "Picking the flies out." Needless to say, on the way home, I found out about the raisins, and every time I have raisin bread, I think of those flies.

We were coming home one day, and as we came close to the Larson place, we saw a fire. It was in a haystack. The Larson kids had got firecrackers for the fourth of July, and one of them went into the haystack. John Thompson came and put a cable around the stack and pulled it away from the barn with his Model A car. You can bet the kids never got anymore firecrackers.

Uncle John also used the Model A to pull hay up at our farm. We had what you call, a stacker. It had two poles on each side and was bolted together on top, a cable between them, and a "dead man" buried in the ground to hold them upright. A carriage ran on the cable and the forks came down on the load of hay. You set the forks, and when you pull on the other end, the forks go up to the carriage. Then the carriage would go down the cable to wherever you wanted the hay. Then you tripped the forks, and they went back for another load. This time, John couldn't pull it up, so he took a run for it, and down came the stacker poles and all. That just missed me by inches. I don't think I have to tell you, but it was off limits when they hayed after that.

One of the best things we did, was to slide down a haystack in the winter. But always on a side away from the house, so Dad couldn't see us. We even trained our dog Jip to climb up the ladder so he could slide down with us. Old Jip was the best dog anyone could have. One day, he came home sick, from bad food or something. Maybe poison. He died later that day. We buried him by the big willow tree where the big blue rock was that could be our castle, ship, or whatever we were playing.

There was a time I was nine years old on the ninth of April. Everyone said it was my lucky birthday. I never saw anything special about it. Then the next year in 1944, the Banyais had a baby, and everybody said it was my birthday present. Wow! No one I ever knew got a birthday present. So we went to see him. He was all wrinkly and hollering, so I said to mother, "Let's leave him here for a while. He looks like too much work." So Peter was born, now called Pastor Pete.

When we wanted to go to town, Dad hitched up the horses and wagon. This would happen in the spring when the roads would break up sometimes. We had to take turns hauling milk cans over to County J or Highway 8, about three miles away. The time I remember was a nice spring day. Dad had put hay in the wagon box, and he and mother sat on the seat in front. We went up over Heacock's Hill over to County J. We saw other farms and families, but mostly nothing but woods and roads. Soon we would lay on our backs in the straw and watch the clouds and sky go by. Soon we were asleep. We came to Bader's store and there was a rail to tie up the horses. We went in the store. OH! What a place. I was in a store! I was never in a store before, and I was almost eight years old! I saw cookies and more cookies. Mother bought us each a soft cookie with black and white stripes. We called them skunk cookies for as long as I can remember. Back home we went, talking about our adventure in the big town. When we got home, it was evening. They milked the cows hurriedly, and everyone crawled to bed early, excited from a tiring day.

Dad was a good hunter from his younger days and army training. One time it didn't pay off. He saw a nice deer south of the house by the cows' salt block. Dad thought we needed some fresh meat, so he grabbed his gun and crawled into a lilac bush to aim and shoot. He aimed, shot, and missed. The deer didn't know where it came from, so it ran right for the lilac bush. Dad shot again and missed the deer, again! The deer almost ran over him, and went into the garden. He shot again and missed. The deer danced around a little bit and ran into the woods. Dad just couldn't understand how he could miss a deer three times! We teased him for a long time about the deer almost running over him. Some time later, we found out that the gun was Andrew's, and his brother John and Slim Barbeau wanted a short outlaw gun, so they cut six inches off the barrel, so when a bullet came through, it would go one way or the other. Those boys never told what they did, they just brought it back to our place until the day Dad used it and almost got ran over by a deer.

Chores? Yes, we had those. The girls did the dishes, but we hauled in the water, the wood, and cut rutabagas every night to feed the cows. Dad always raised a couple acres of them every year, and then after the frost, he would cut off the tops and put them in the cellar, and then every day we would cut them up to take to the cows for feed. One time I had to help Bernice wash dishes. Not my favorite chore. Of course she had to tease me about it, so I took off my shoe and threw it at her. I missed, and right through the window it went. Boy, was I in trouble. It broke a nice hole in one corner and Dad put an old glass picture over it, and it stayed that way until we moved. Just a reminder to me I think.

Dad never hit us, all he did was look at us with his clear blue eyes, and that was enough. Mother very seldom spanked us. There was a switch above the door. It must've been used for Garey.

In the summertime, we had to walk to the mailbox which was a mile away, and we had to be sure not to lose anything. My sister Adelaide always, and I mean ALWAYS wrote a letter home on Sunday. She sent it out on Monday from Wakefield, Michigan, and we got it on Wednesday. If it didn't come, Mother would ask us, "Are you SURE you didn't lose it?"

One day, we were waiting for mail, and we heard Lyle Cronk had a baby, so we walked over to see her. She was crying and her tongue looked square on the end, so I told Garey, "That's why babies can't talk. Their tongues haven't grown out yet." Pretty smart wasn't I? One other time, we were waiting for mail, and were climbing trees. I climbed an old Basswood tree and wanted to get up to the top. I wanted it to bend down, and the branch cracked and I fell head first into the ditch. I could taste blood for two or three days, but never went to the doctor. Maybe this explains a lot of things.

We had our sad times too. Our neighbor, Mrs. Rogalla had a baby boy, and she died afterwards. She was laid out to rest in the living room of her house with a bible in her hands and a rosary. Very sad. Mr. Rogalla was left with two little boys to raise.

The first person I ever saw dead was Grace Hvass, that was Chris Hvass' girl. They lived across from Harvey Hvass' place. We went to the Methodist church in Kennan to see her. A young lady. When I was about eight years old, Grandpa Thompson died. The last I saw him alive, he was carrying a rocking chair over to our place on his back. Our son Tom now has that chair. Then he went to Park Falls to what they called a rest home. He didn't have any money, so the county took care of him and took his home. When he died, Dad bought the house and eighty acres for $350. He was buried in Kennan. Hugo Kandutsch was the undertaker. We went to his viewing place, and they played The Old Rugged Cross on a wind up phonograph player. Then to church. They would only take him into the hallway, because he didn't have any money and was not a paid up member. Right there I lost my religion. Here was a nice old man, who never hurt anyone, and because he didn't pay his dues, he had to stay in the hall and not in the front of the church. I remember Uncle John took it real hard too. He cried so much. I don't remember Andrew being home, which was not unusual. He would sit at the kitchen table with us and talk, and then not be home for dinner! Then six months or so later, he would come home, and in a little while he would go again. Maybe a year or more would pass before he'd come back again. Sometimes, he'd write, sometimes, he wouldn't. No one seemed to worry about him.

Before I could remember, Fairview school had preachers that would come and hold revivals there, because it was too far to go to church, and there were so many different religions at the time in the community. A preacher got the crowd worked up real good and one of the neighbor ladies had the Spirit come upon her, and she said, "The last child I had was not my husband's but my brother's." Wasn't long they said, and she was gone with all the kids. The husband stayed here all his life and died here.

Dad came in for dinner one day and said, "Annie, I gotta set a trap by them peas. A woodchuck must be eating them." Garey and I knew what was eating them. Boy, we thought we were pretty clever. Now, I think Dad knew all along who the woodchuck was. He never did set any traps for the "real" woodchuck.

Dad was born a German-Jew. With a name like Pfaffendorf, what else could he be? In World War Two, some boys in the

neighborhood called him Hitler the Kraut.
Well, somehow that got back to their dad, and
he marched them up to our place and they had
to apologize. As these boys grew up, we
became real good friends with them, and they
were related to us later, so it turned out okay.

One winter, my dad was sick a lot. He
mentioned it to our neighbors, Mr. and Mrs.
John Figura. She got out a jar of herbs and told
her husband John how to take it, because she
did not speak good English. So John told my
Dad how to take it. Dad took it for a while and
felt better. It had cured him. Then he told John

about it. "Yeah," John said, "Mary used it on a horse that was sick one time, and it got better too." The Figuras were good neighbors, but in the fall, when the garden was ready to harvest, their cows came right into the garden, Dad's pride and joy. That was not a good time to be around.

In about 1947, my dad took a load of manure out on a sleigh with his horses. A white mustang named Birdy and her son, Prince. As he spread manure, the horses bolted and ran away, hitting his shoulder and breaking it. I remember him sitting on the cot with the bones sticking out of his shoulder, wondering if he should go to the doctor. Mother walked down to Charlie Heacock's, about two miles south and asked him to take Dad to Kennan. as he always had a good car and was always helping the neighbors. He came and got Dad and took him to Kennan to Otto Keller, who was also a World War One veteran. Keller helped a lot of veterans. Then he took him to Prentice to the doctor, and they put a harness on his arm and put him on a train to Milwaukee all by himself. There were no painkillers back then, so it must've been a long ride. Then he had to walk from the train to the vet's hospital. He was gone for six weeks. We were all alone. George Erickson, who was the mailman and milkman, and the neighbors helped out with getting food and whatever else we needed. Six weeks later, a car came in the driveway. Mother said, "Here comes your dad. I can tell by the size of his ears." Dad came in, sat down, and cried. That was the first and last time I ever saw him do that. He was so happy to be home, and we were happy to see him.

I can tell you something else, and you can believe it or not, but I know it happened, because I was there. It was the middle of winter, I remember, because all three of us kids were sleeping downstairs. We had a brown leather couch that folded out to make a bed. All of us kids slept there, me in the middle. It was a quiet moonlit night, and I was awoken by a noise. I looked up, and there walking through the house was a beautiful girl with blonde hair, wearing a beautiful nightgown. Now I know it wasn't a nightgown, it was a long dress. Then I thought it was a nightgown. I'd never seen one before. She looked at me, smiled and laughed. Her laughter was like a glass bell ringing. Then she walked over to the stairway and disappeared. There was a door there, but she never opened it. She was very beautiful. I knew she was my Grandma

Thompson. Even my mother had never seen her, because she had died within a week of my mother's birth. No one knew much about her except Grandpa. He never mentioned it, because he was remarried, and they didn't talk about that. I never told anybody about it until after I got married. No one would believe me.

I started doing family history to look for her. I found where she lived, and that she was buried in St. Paul. Finally after my retirement, I had enough time to work on the computer. I looked for her, and there are only 163 Karen Andersens that came to America. Just lately, I received a picture from my sister that I had never seen. There she was, as I had seen her years ago. I hired a Mormon lady to help me search records. We thought we had found her several different times, but it just didn't fit. Finally, in 2001, we found her, her father, brother, and some of her family. Now we are waiting for the priest in that town to look into her books to see if there are any living descendants of her brother's who are still living there. I hope to someday tell this story to one of them.

My Grandmother Karen Margaret Andersen

[confirmation picture]

As I mentioned before, my dad was not the world's fastest car driver. Or the best. Mother always said that Dad thought the radiator cap should be on the yellow line. One Memorial Day, we had a Reo car, and we were going to Kennan for services, so Dad could march in the parade. The car started to fill up with smoke. About two miles later we found out that the emergency brake was on. Then there was the time Dad stopped right in front of a semi truck. The driver told him how to drive and where to park the old Reo. In 2002, Don Lebal told me about the time he was hauling milk, and Dad pulled right out in front of him on the

Highway. Don missed him by going into the ditch and then back on the road. There was no damage. Dad never went over fifteen miles an hour. Finally, when he was about sixty five, he sold the old Reo to Fritz Lebal to make a tractor out of it. Fritz had a great time with it. He drove all over with his puddle jumper.

1946 was the last year I went to Fairview school. In the fall of 1947, I started at the Four Corners School. The reason for that was that my mother's brother Andrew had bought a place on Highway 8, three miles south of us, when he was in the second World war. He was sent to Alaska to work on the Alaskan highway, because he was forty-five years old, too old to be fighting in the real army. After the war, he went to Oregon and worked in the shipyards. One day, we got a telegram that he was found dead in his room. He laid there about seven days. They said it was his heart, but he had no money on him, and he always carried all the money he had. So Mother and her brother John inherited the place. Dad paid John $2,500 and some tools for his share. Mother said, "Willie, we're going to move down to that place by Highway 8 so the boys can go to High School without staying someplace in town like Adelaide and Bernice did." In April, Dad started moving things down there with the horse and sleigh. Then later, we took four cows down and moved in. There wasn't as much traffic on the roads then as there is now. For about a week, every time a car would go by, Dad would run to see who it was.

I started eighth grade at the Four Corners School. Our teacher's name was Mrs. Coen. One day, Helen Barbeau came down and asked Mrs. Coen to put Garey and I back a grade. Mrs. Coen said, "I can't do that, you gave them all A's and B's last year, so you figure it out."

What was wrong with her? I don't know. The

Four Corners was a nice school. I met new kids

there, who were my friends for many years.

A little bit about my parents, my dad,

William Frederick Pfaffendorf, had come from

Minnesota. His dad, Herman Henry

Pfaffendorf, had given him a horse and buggy,

the only way to get home was to drive it, so he

started out. It took him three days to get home.

He had feed and hay for his horse. Every time

he stopped, someone would feed them and put

them up for the night. When he got home, he

had more feed than when he started. When my dad and mother, Anna Catherine Thompson, came to homestead their farm in Wisconsin, there was only a trail that ran from the school to their place, so they built up on the hill. They put in a well, and then came the road. It was about forty acres across the way, so they decided to move closer to it. They used horses and a stump puller. It took about two weeks.

I do believe they had the first mobile home in the family. One day, before they moved the house, Dad walked to Kennan, which took most of the day. He got a big bologna sausage

Anna and William Pfaffendorf

My mother and father taken about 1940's at

Alvin Sitan's place

and a pail of syrup. He was coming home, and it was dark as he made his way up the trail. He heard a wolf howl close by, and in a hurry to get away, he tripped over a log and lost his food. You could see him in the moonlight, trying to find his food, and the wolf getting closer. He was glad to get home. He showed us many times, the big blue rock by the road. The rock still sits there today.

Things were not easy for my parents. Once, they needed a cow, so Dad went to work in the woods all winter. He came home in the spring and the banks went broke. The banker and his wife lived in Kennan for many years and never worked again. The second year, he brought the money home with him and bought a cow. Five weeks later, she got out and into the clover patch, bloated, and died. The third winter, he made it and got another cow.

Adelaide told me about the time Mother was pregnant with Bernice, and Mother passed out. Here was a young girl, all by herself in the woods. What could she do? Finally, Mother came to and was okay.

Years ago, when my mother and dad lived up north yet, when we were all still young, my parents would drive three miles with the horse and us kids. Dad would play his violin for the school house dances. Many people came from miles around to dance there. Us kids would fall asleep on the benches, and be covered up with coats until it was time to go home. I wish I could remember some of those rides home. I'm sure there would have been some interesting tales.

I remember when I was young, and we lived up north, close to the Fairview school,

Mother would butcher about a dozen chickens, put them in a pack sack, put them on her back, and walk to Catawba, so she could exchange them for food. She also took eggs if she had them. Every place took eggs for grocery bills. That was about fifteen miles round trip.

Dad once told me about the time he came from the woods, and stopped at Wick's store on the way home, and bought two dollars worth of fish. He said he could hardly carry it. Those were the good old days.

In the 1940's sometime, Adelaide got married, and Dad's sister Mary and her husband, George Furman and daughter Lorna Mae came for the reception. They had an old truck, and had made a house on the back, like a mobile home. They had wrote "Happy Newlyweds" on the back of the truck. On the way home, their girl rode in front with her dad, and everywhere they stopped, everyone said, "Happy Newlyweds!" They were father and daughter and everyone thought they were married. About a year later, we received a telegram saying that George and Mary were dead. George had shot Mary and then himself.

At the funeral, both of their dads got into a fight about who killed who. That was not a good time.

Let me tell you about some of the good bee stings I've got in my lifetime. One day, I was walking along barefoot in the clover, and BANG! A big old bumblebee stung me on the big toe. That toe got to be about half as big as my whole foot. Oh, did that hurt! Dad always had bees. One day I was out inspecting them, and I poked a stick in the hive so they would come out. And did they come out! They got me between the eyes. One eye swelled up. I looked like a little china man. The kids at school sure had a good time laughing at me.

In the old days at Christmas time, my dad would go find a Charlie Brown tree someplace. It usually had five branches on the whole thing. We would set it up Christmas Eve and trim it. We had some old bulbs that Grandpa Thompson had given us, and we strung popcorn, and we also ate a lot of it too. For lights, we had little clips that you put candles in and then put on the tree. Then Mother would light them and we had to sit real still. Any breeze would make them flicker and might cause a fire. As we sat like two little mice, Dad would sit over in the corner and play his violin while he sang old Christmas songs like, Old Tannenbaum, Silent Night, and sometimes he would sing When The Moon Went Over The Cattle Shed and Miss Froggy Went A Courting. Oh, just to hear those songs again.

There was an old lady that lived in our neighborhood named Mrs. Ryan. She was about eighty years old, and she had been burned real bad in the face, and had disfigured her. But, at eighty, she was going around the neighborhood looking for clothes for her baby that was coming. Now this was before Viagra. Wow, huh!?!

One day, Garey and I got to talking as kids do, about money. It seemed our parents were always poor. So we thought, let's plant some pennies and grow our own money. Like corn, we planted and watered it, but no money came. We were still broke. Those pennies are still buried there today.

As Garey and I played in our driveway one time, we heard an awful racket. We looked up and here comes Dad's team of horses. They had run away with the spring tooth behind them. We had made it out of the way just in time. I swear I could feel their chin whiskers.

One winter day, I believe it was the day Jerry Sokolowski broke his arm swinging on the rafters in the woodshed. Anyways, our teacher, Miss. Joy Soetebeer went someplace, so the kids were left alone at school. The boys were outside having a snowball fight. Of course, the girls had to open the windows and tease us. Soon the snowballs were flying inside and everything was wet. For some reason, my brother was inside too. We were having great fun, then I looked down the road, about half a mile away, and here comes Dad at his smart clip of fifteen miles an hour. I ran out to the boys' bathroom, and he stopped since he was on the School Board and wanted to know where the teacher was. Someone told him that she left. All the time I was out there thinking they would send me to a boys' home or something like that. After he left, we cleaned it up fast. I don't know if the teacher ever knew about it. Dad never said a word and Garey never told on me either. Was that my lucky day.

When the winter days were real nice, we would go sliding on Heacock Hill to the east of the school. Now that was fun. One person would belly flop on the sled and start down the hill. Part way down, someone else would jump on top and lay down. Then the third one would jump on. If we were too top heavy, we would run into the ditch or tip over. But, if everything went as planned, we would go clipping down the hill and halfway up the next. Everyone walking up the hill threw snowballs at us. We would work real hard to get our work done, so we could go sliding at noon.

Our lunch was in an old syrup pail by the stove to keep it warm. No hot meals in those days. No lunch meat or goodies, only bread with butter and jam or syrup on it. We were hard on our lunch pails, we hit everything with them.

The show house in Hawkins was a wonderful place to go as a young kid. The movies were nice. Mr. Zeilke would make all the kids be quiet or out you went. Orland and Bernice took us most of the time. It was twenty- five cents per show. We had to search through all the pants for that kind of money.

One time we found twenty cents in Dad's church pants. That helped. Orland had a 1935 Ford and when it rained, he put a string on the wipers and pulled them by hand. But, we got there and back. One time, Garey and I were going fishing with Orland. He was teasing Bernice and she got mad, so she threw a whole pail of water right in the car window. No sense of humor.

Up on the Ryder's place, by Seth Stevenson's, there was a pond and a creek. Mostly mud and really deep. Me, Garey, and the Hvass boys (Jack and Buddy) would go there. There was an old boat in real bad shape, so I sank it so no one would drown in there. Buddy didn't like that at all. So what were we to do? We went to Kennan Lumber for boat building supplies, because Dad was working at the saw mill. We just charged everything to him. All of it was tongued and grooved lumber. We started to build like mad before payday, when Dad would find out that we charged it to him. Well, we didn't make it. He really wasn't mad, he just told us to be sure it was safe. Then he told us that when he was a kid, he went upstairs in his dad's house, where they had seasoned lumber for special projects, and he made an airplane out of some wood. That didn't go good either. It must run in the family, because our oldest boy Lonnie cut up my Baptismal Certificate to make an airplane. You just can't replace that.

Dad's brother Ernest, and his family, would come up to visit. They also liked to fish. We went down to the Jump River, south of Kennan. You couldn't drive in then, so we just parked on County N. Ernest had brought peaches one time and they sure tasted good, especially when you're hungry and have no fish to fry. We also went north of Hawkins to

The cousins back on the old Pfaffendorf farm

back row: Marion, Bernice, Dan

front row: Wilbur, Garey, Eldorine, Larry,

Melvin

the Flambeau River. Nice Strawberry Bass up there, and lots of Pine snakes. When we went there, there was no bridge, so you only went to the river. We went with Uncle John one time, and there was a snake that was from ditch to ditch long. I remember that with his Model A car, he ran over it, and there was a bump. Then he backed up and spun the wheels on it. He said, "If you get the skin off a snake, they'll die from sunburn. On the same day, we saw a man that caught a big fish that was laying in the back seat of a Model A. It took up the whole seat! People that went up to Connor's Lake had to ford the river. Alvin Sitan, our old neighbor, was always ready to fish. We would tie our cane poles on to Orland Peterson's car, and away we went. Sometimes by Shamrock Lake by Hawkins to get Bullheads at night, or to the Jump River, or Flambeau. One time, Garey and I were with and we wanted to go home, but Alvin would say, "Hold it, I got a nibble!" We snuck around through the bushes and woods and got his can of worms and dumped them. He couldn't figure out how they all got out. He sure loved to fish. Sometimes, Bernice's girls, Mary and Sue, would go with. Alvin had an old horse named Prince. Orland and I would borrow Prince to skid out firewood. One day, as we worked, he just up and died. So we had to take the harness off and tell Alvin that old Prince was dead. He just said, "He was old, you can expect that." Nowadays, people would say, "You have to pay for that horse, or we'll sue you!"

Everyone knew the Sitans. They always had a great garden and were always giving things from it to people. Alvin had an apple tree by the well. He called then Well apples, and he would guard that tree until they got ripe. They were the best apples I ever ate. I would give anything for one more of those Well apples.

Mother had only one cousin in the United States. She had more in Denmark, but never corresponded with them. This cousin was Mary Thompson. She came many times to visit. She was a big, raw-boned lady. Very kind and full of fun. She was also the first person I knew who talked about and actually got equal rights for women. She had one daughter, Janice Hoogland who married Wes Filkins and they had two girls, who are also married now and have children. They live in northern Minnesota.

When we rode the bus to Phillips High School, we went on lot of back roads. In the winter time, there was a lot of snow, and sometimes we got stuck. Herman Seeger was our bus driver. He said, "Okay boys, get out and push." So when he went ahead, we held back. When he backed up, we pushed ahead. We thought that was fun. Poor Mr. Seeger had a hard time with us kids, but he lived to be over ninety, so we didn't hurt him. Of course, if he wouldn't have drove bus, maybe he would have lived to be a hundred and twenty, who knows. Can you even imagine what would happen nowadays if you told the boys to go out and push the bus? There would be some big lawsuits there.

Friends of mine, Bruce Noller and Clarence Esteimer, who we called Outlaw, went to Catechism with me. Boy, that was a bunch. Clarence got killed in a car accident as a young man out west. Bruce had it made, he went out west and married a rancher's daughter. The only daughter they had. One night, he robbed a gas station and killed a man. He spent a lot of years in prison. In high school, he rode our bus, and was always in trouble. I remember he got kicked off the bus by Hvass' about three miles from home and he had to walk. The day before hunting season, he came over. He had a gun, so we went way up north in our woods, and did target practicing. Then we checked traps and came home. When he went to cross the highway to get to his house, there was a game warden. They put him in the car and came over for me. I told him that I was just out checking my traps. He said, "Okay, let's see your license." You guessed it, I didn't have one. So he gave us a speech about no guns before deer season and no traps with out a license. He said, "I'm going to let you boys go." Were we happy! He said, "I'll take Bruce home and talk to his grandmother, and you, Lawrence, go pull out those traps. You should have seen me scoot around that trap line. I was home in no time. Orland and Bernice were there at the time. They thought it was funny, but I sure didn't.

Bruce came back several times. One time, he robbed Wick's store for some shoes. Those were the kind of kids I hung around with. He was a good kid most of the time. His mother lived somewhere in the cities, and his grandmother raised him. One day, our little bus was headed for Phillips, I was playing cards and all of a sudden all the kids were screaming. The back wheel came off and we went in the ditch. Good thing old Herman had a hold on it. We just played more cards, and let him worry how we would get to school.

Once, I had an appointment to go see a doctor. I got a shot once a week, and he said, "Stay away from pop and sweets." On the way back to school, you guessed it, I stopped at the sweet shop for pop. They had a drink called Mississippi Mud. They mixed every kind together.

Phillips High School had a janitor named Jim Zeman, who was our classmate, Gloria Zeman's father. Part of his job was to plow the sidewalks. He had an old puddle jumper with a plow on the front. He would back up and take a run for the snow. We would play chicken to see who could stay the longest in the way. He would of course slow down so he wouldn't hit us. Then he ran out of power and had to back up for another run. We made life hard for him.

We had a lot of tough kids in school, but no one was like Johnny Gang. He was only in sixth or seventh grade, and the big high school boys would try to take the baseball bat away from him. Boy, he sure could put up a fight.

My dad was road boss in our little community. One day, Ray Ryder, who lived down the road, came over and said, "Bill, could you give me some work on the road? We don't have any flour or food for the children." Dad said, "Sure, take a shovel and open up the ditch from your place to the creek." That was about a quarter of a mile. So Ray went happily to work. Then he came back and asked, "Bill, could I borrow some boots from you?" So he did his job and got paid. He said, "God bless

Uncle Bill." Dad wasn't really an uncle, but my mother's brother was married to Ray's sister Martha.

Free shows were held in Kennan and Catawba on most Saturday nights in the summertime to get the farmers to come in and shop. A sheet was put up on the south side of Esteimer Hall in Kennan. In Catawba, on the west side of the feed mill, behind Wick's store. By today's standards, they were poor movies. One time, two guys were in the French foreign legion. They had KP and had to wash clothes. They put them on a pyramid, and started on the bottom and worked up, so they walked all over the clean clothes every time they put more clothes on. Then they put them in the guard house, and the last you saw them, they were playing the bed springs and singing, "If I Had The Wings Of An Angel." It was the only social thing we had, so Dad would say, "You boys do your chores, and we will go to the show." But, as he finished up his night chores, he might say, "I'm just too tired to go." We never could understand that, but I sure do now.

For Christmas dinner, we always had bread pudding. It tasted so good. No one makes it like your mother does. My mother also had Fattigmand. It was a pie crust rolled out with powdered sugar on it. Some years before my time, my grandma and grandpa Pfaffendorf would send my parents a dressed out chicken. Can you believe they sent a chicken through the mail? Today they wouldn't carry a chicken would they?

Then there was the Ladies' Aid. This was a bunch of women from the Lutheran church in Kennan. Each one would take turns holding the meeting. We loved this when mother had her turn. Always in the summertime. They had big bologna lunch meat, was that good, not like now. White buns, (We had dark bread most of the time at home.) and maybe a cinnamon roll. I sure wish us boys could've had food like that everyday. Instead we had salt pork, chicken, and lots of greens. When the garden was ready, we ate high on the hog. Tomatoes, carrots, and all those good things. One time, Doris McCombs came with her mother and we showed her the whole farm. Little did I know that some day, she would be my sister-in-law and stand up for my wedding.

Joe Figura was a good friend and was older than me. One day at school we came in with wet mittens and I threw Joe's off the stove pipe so I could have room for mine. Just plain mean wasn't it? Well, Joe didn't like that arrangement, so he pushed me down on the floor and sat on me. Jimmy Ryder was an older boy and he pulled Joe off of me. It was my fault, but Joe got roughed up for it. Life wasn't always fair. That was the only fight I had in eight years of grade school, so that's not too bad. Joe had a broken nose from something, so he was called Broken Nose Figura. I don't know why they called him that. He had two older brothers named Mike and Bill. Those boys could do anything. They built puddle jumpers, did well drilling, and later, Bill started to make an all-terrain vehicle. It was a special kind, and they still produce them today. Nancy Figura came and took care of Mother when Garey was born. Later, I helped her parents, John and Mary hay after everyone left home. They were a good family and good friends.

When we were young, at Christmas time, the older boys from the fifth grade or so who had their work done and had been good, were chosen to go get the Christmas tree. I bet you're wondering how I ever got on that detail. Well, I did. We would start out with an ax. We went Indian style, single file. We could go anywhere for a tree, no one cared. There was no posted land. We looked at a lot of trees, but we needed that perfect one. Soon we spotted it. The only problem was, that it was on the top of a thirty foot tall tree. So what! We could do it. We took turns chopping it down. You could hear the ax as it bit into the Fir tree. Down it came. We were so disappointed. It wasn't nearly as perfect as it looked way up there. Oh, look! It's about three o'clock. So we had to hurry to school before it was time to go home. Would you believe it, there on the way back was a perfect tree right by the road.

The Aladdin lamp that lit the school was turned down on the night of the Christmas play. Along with the candles burning brightly, and the paper chains we had all made, you could hear the moms and dads say, "Oh, it's so beautiful!" Then we knew we had really gotten the perfect Christmas tree.

Do I believe in Santa Claus? Oh yes! I saw him for real when I was real little. One

Christmas Eve, Santa knocked on our door. There he was saying, "Merry Christmas!" He brought me a plane you could wind up and fly. I suppose it was one of the neighbor boys, but I never asked about it, and no one ever told me.

One other time with nothing to do at school, some of us boys went across the road to a little white house that Lawrence Graham had. No one lived in it, so we had to get in and find out what was in there. We found a window that wasn't locked, so we crawled in and looked around. We needed something. Finally, we found it. A gallon of green paint. We stole it and hid it in the woods. We never did find it again. Charlie Graham came to school, and all the kids blamed Joe Figura. He never denied it, so he took the blame for it. Joe was a great kid, but everyone picked on him because he spoke Polish at home, and school was hard for him. He always said, "I got up this morning and shoed myself." We thought that was funny. Joe got a bicycle one year, so he gave me a ride part way, then went back and got Garey, and took him ahead, then came back and got me, and so it went, all the way home. His dad said, "I buy bike for Joey to get home sooner, and it takes him longer!"

We had to try to stop and dam up the creek until one time, there was a wooden plank bridge on the road over the creek. I was underneath playing, and something went down my neck. I looked, and there was a snake, dead, but caught between the planks. Boy did I scream and run for home. I never went back under there again.

One time, Garey and I built a nice little igloo snow house. We put boards on top and put snow and ice on the walls and everything. It was so nice. Then Garey did something that made me mad. I chased him, and he ran over top of the igloo. He was lighter than me, and I came after him and right down I went. Then we had to rebuild the whole top of the igloo. That was a good one too. Even Jip, our dog, slept in it on cold winter nights. When we were doing this work, Garey got too close, and I cut him above the eye with the shovel. He still has that scar. I don't know about the ones on the butt though.

The snow plow would plow big drifts. Or at least we thought they were big. When it froze, it was like steel. We dug holes from the top down, and had a nice place. When the Hvass girls or other kids came, we had snowball fights. These holes were wonderful forts. When we were young, the Jehovah's Witnesses would come to save our souls. They came on a bicycle, and had a phonograph that you wind up. They played church music for us and gave us a speech on how life should be. They also had little story books for the kids.

Then there were the fruit peddlers. He had an old truck, and always said, "Lady, I got a good deal for you." Fruit was hard to get, so we always got something. He took chickens, eggs, old junk, anything in trade. Remember I told you about my uncle, Andrew. He would buy anything. One time, the little Jew came with fruit right before the fourth of July. He knew he couldn't sell the cherries, so he offered them to Andrew. A good deal. He couldn't resist, so on the fourth of July, they pitted cherries and canned them. What a job on the fourth of July. I never forgot that.

Dad had a real hard job one time. His favorite horse Prince got real sick and wouldn't eat. He called the vet, and he came and looked at him and said he had lock jaw. There was no cure for that, so Dad had to lead him way over onto the west side of the field and kill him with a hammer. I know it had to hurt Dad real bad. He didn't talk about it until years later.

When I was small, about ten or eleven, my sister Adelaide and her family brought a dog down that they couldn't keep. His name was Boomba Dear. That was a really nice name. He was a Chihuahua, and we became good friends. He slept on my cot. If Garey came, he would growl. Bernice hated him, because she was just starting to date, and when she came home, he would just about tear the linoleum off the floor.

That would wake up Mom and Dad, and they didn't like that. I never told him to be quiet, he was just doing his job. When we went trapping and went to check our trap line, I'd put him in my pack sack with his little head sticking out. He liked that. But, all good things come to an end, and one day as Dad drove briskly down the driveway, Boomba Dear ran down the road and slipped, and Dad ran over him. He felt as bad as I did. We buried him between the horse barn and the granary.

For fun one day while Mom and Dad went to town, Garey and I hatched a plan. Bernice was scrubbing the linoleum floor in the house, and we knew that she was afraid of chickens, so we caught our rooster and opened the door, and in he went on the nice clean floor. You could hear her scream for about five miles. In a little while, she opened the door and out came old Henry the rooster, proud as could be.

We picked on Bernice a lot, but she had it coming. One time, she was all ready to go out on a date, so she went down to say goodbye to the folks. Pretty soon, we had gotten her mad and she chased us out the barn door, and up the planks where Dad wheeled the manure. She slipped. Right into the manure she went. She looked and smelled terrible. Us boys had jumped on top of the flat little barn roof. We harassed her as she ran to the house to clean up and change. You bet we were laughing.

Our old chicken coop was run over with mice so we went down there with our BB guns and sat there in the dark. The mice would come from all over to get to the feeder. One of us would turn on the light and the other one would fire at will. I think we shot more chickens than mice. In about an hour, we found out there was lice in there too.

Before I was born, there was a man named Williams who lived across from where Frank and Josephine Lazar now live. He was a real mean man. His wife had to walk to town and carry 50 pounds of flour home for them. They had a family. He beat her and the kids. She showed people at his wake where he had shot at her by the door frame. One day he was dead. He was cleaning out some hides and he died. People were sure that she had poisoned him, but no one cared. In those days, some one sat with the body all night until it could be buried. Dad was one of the lucky ones that night. The next day, they took him by wagon and buried him in Kennan. Dad said the hole was full of water, but in it he went in his box. He was buried on the Lutheran side where the big Spruce tree is now.

When Mother and Dad got married, they moved in with my dad's parents in Minnesota. They had five boys and one girl and almost everybody was gone. Each one had their own bedroom upstairs. Mother was new to the farm, and they had a big German Sheperd dog. The dog had buried some bones under the shed. Mother went over there for something and he thought that she was after his food, so he attacked her. She had over a hundred and fifty bite marks on her arms. They wrapped her up and took her to town. Dr. Terpania sewed her up and did a real good job. You could see some marks but not much. About thirty-five years later, she stepped in his office when she was back visiting. The doctor said, "Sure I remember you! But, I suppose the dog is dead by now." They didn't kill the dog because they felt he was just protecting his food.

Mother said she never went to school until she was nine years old, because her dad and stepmother moved so much. He rented farmhouses, and they lived in houses that no one was using, but sometimes, they did want to use them, so they just moved on. She said her stepmother was very good to her. Grandpa and his second wife had one son named John. Her step mother must've been good, because my mother named her first child, Adelaide, after her. Grandma Thompson's name was Adelaide Mortenson. Her father put elevators in old St. Paul buildings. Her brother Art sold real estate. They were well to do. They never liked my grandpa. When old Mr. Mortenson died, he gave his grandson John five dollars in his will.

One time, they were up to see the family in a new Pontiac car in about 1925. they took Mom, Dad, Adelaide, and Grandma Adelaide for a ride. Adelaide got carsick and threw up in the car. She wasn't too popular for quite a while.

There was a lady in the neighborhood who loved to go riding. If a car went, she was in it. Dad said one day, "I hope you run out of gas someday and have to walk home." A little while later, guess who was out riding in the same car with that lady. Right, my dad, and sure enough, they ran out of gas and he had to

walk.

My Mother's Father and Mother
Michael Christian Chobyln Thompson and
Karen Margaret Andersen. Married March 28,
1898.

My Great Grandparents

Andrew Martin Thompson and Karen Madsen

Married March 26, 1859.

One time, he went to try to get another one of the neighbors to go fight forest fires. He refused. Dad said, "I hope your place burns down, and no one comes to help you." It wasn't a month later and his house burned down. The first place the sheriff went was to see old Willie Pfaffendorf, but he had a good alibi.

As I woke up one morning, a beautiful day was dawning. As I slowly came out of my sleep, I became aware that today, I was a TEENAGER! Wow! Teenagers can do anything. Wrong! I found out that you can't do

ANYTHING! You're too young to smoke and drink, and even to young to drive a car. That's how I felt a thirteen years old, but life goes on.

In our teens, we did some pretty nasty things. My brother Garey's favorite things were cats. He HATED them! We had a small barn with a hayloft, and we had a small hole in the loft where we threw down the baled hay. Well, Garey would go up from the outside and close the trap door. All the cats knew him, and as soon as he came in the barn, they would jump on the stantions above the cows, and up through the trap door. Now the trap door is closed, but the cats don't know it. So when he comes running into the barn, the cats spring for the hole, and boom, bang, down they fall, knocked out cold, and Garey is jumping with glee.

Mother always favored Garey, since he was the baby of the family and all. One time, Garey and his friend, Jack Hvass, drank a quart of wine they got someplace. Boy, did they get sick. Mother said, "Poor Garey, he must've eaten too many of those porkchops" Their room smelled like a winery. I said to him, "How's it going?" He said, "My bed keeps trying to go up the wall. Ohhhh, here it goes again!"

One other time when we were in our teens, our dad was planting grapes to make an arbor, and who should come, but some Jehovah's Witnesses. They stopped and talked to Dad. One man said, "Today is Sunday, you shouldn't be planting things and working." Well, my dad was a little on the stubborn side. Well, maybe more than a little. He told them, "These are my grapes, this is my land, and I will plant them when and where I want to." The man said, "You'll never get any grapes on those vines with that attitude. It is fifty years later, and the vines are still there, and we are still waiting for our first crop.

It wasn't long, and it was time to start high school. That was a big move for me. I started to figure out that there was a lot of things out there to try. There was the big bus trip to the Hawkins school, five miles away. I was never on a bus before, that was new to me. We were more or less coming out of the Dark ages. In order to be part of the Hawkins gang, we had to be initiated. Another new thing. "What is it?" I thought. I soon found out. They told us that each of us had to dress so that we would stand out so everyone could tell we were freshmen. They gave us a piece of paper on what to wear. Some got long underwear, some had to leave their hair uncombed. I slowly opened mine, dreading the worst. Oh No! It was the worst! It said, dress like a girl. Oh God, what did I ever do to deserve this? Maybe it was the calf riding, the BB guns, or one of the other times I was mean to my little brother. But, if you gotta, you gotta. So I got a dress from my sister, and Mother put a perm in my hair with one of those old irons, and Monday morning, I was ready to go. There were some men working on Highway 8, and they gave me the eye. I must've looked kinda cute. I hid in the bushes so no one else would see me. When I got on the bus, the bus driver laughed so hard he could hardly drive. I knew right there, it was going to be a LONG day. More of my friends came on the bus, and everyone had a good laugh. In school, it was a day of harassment for us. To top it off, we had a ball game that day, and all the freshmen had to go and sit in the grandstands, and everybody laughed at us. I thought, "Wait 'till next year, when we can initiate the freshmen." That day, I got a new nickname that some still call me today. Curly.

Because of my nice curly hair that day. Now I was part of the gang. We played basketball and baseball. We had a great time. It was such a small school that we had four subjects per year. We needed sixteen to graduate. So if you failed one class, there was no way to make it up. I found out real quick that if you were in sports, your marks were always good. Well, mine weren't that hot. I found other things too. Girls! There was one I liked real well, but I was from a poor family and no education, and didn't have a car. It wasn't long and I was history.

I went two years to Hawkins school, then they consolidated schools in Price county, so the third year, I had to go all the way to Phillips. Now life began for sure! I sold a heifer my dad had given me, and bought my first car. A beautiful 1939 Ford, black as midnight. Now I had wheels. Things were really looking up. I didn't have a driver's license, so I applied for them. I was fifteen and drove, but I never got my regular license until I was twenty-one and married. A lot of miles were put on with out a driver's license. I wonder how I made it. I had a car, so I was everybody's buddy. I got a job as a janitor at the Four Corners school. Man, things were really coming together.

We went roller skating all over. At Hawkins, Ogema, Jump River, and Catawba. One of my friends was Bill Schoenfelder. We drank a little beer and we thought we were hot stuff! At that time, there was a dance hall and a bar down the road from us, and if you went around back and you were tall enough to put your money on the bar, you could buy beer. I never had a taste for it. Never cared for it.

Other kids had cars in town too, and we would play hide-and-seek through the back-alley. Lights out and no street light. Some of the boys hit parked cars, but we were lucky that no one was ever hurt. One time, Garey and I were driving down by the Rusk county line and fooling around. I was driving, and Garey was sitting on the passenger's side. I pushed him and he hit the door handle, and out he went. I thought I had killed him for sure. When I stopped and ran back, he got up. You could see the tire track on his blue jean jacket. That was close. I think I hugged him.

Roller skating was a lot of fun, and a good way to meet new kids. We had a lot of fun. We never got in fights, but there were some kids that did. There were always girls to talk to, and most of them were very nice people. We also drank a little beer, and smoked a couple cigarettes. No drugs or sex in those days. I had another friend that I ran around with. Chuck Perdum. Some guy he was. He had a girlfriend, and about this time, I fell in love for the first time. A dark-haired girl started talking to me, and that was the first time I ever started thinking about girls. And this one was great. She changed my life. She called me Larry for the first time. Nobody had ever done that before. I asked her, "What is that?" She said, "It's a nickname for Lawrence." Well praise the Lord, I became Larry forever more. She was also the first girl I ever kissed. I didn't know how it sounded, but I thought it sounded like a cow pulling her foot out of the mud. Not her fault. We practiced a lot and we did okay. She was a good girl and a nice friend. We used to sit and listen to the Del Rio Texas radio station. All country love songs and it came in so good.

One time, me, Chuck, and Dick Heizler went outlawing for deer. We shot one doe and put it in the back seat. We crossed the Jump River south of Kennan in my old Studebaker. Halfway across, there was no bridge, the car flooded out. We were in trouble. But as luck would have it, it started up, and we made it home. At 5:00 in the morning, I crawled into bed for an hour and then had to get up and ready for work.

Bill Schoenfelder, me, and Otto Schoenfelder, Bill's stepfather, went shining one night for deer. We saw a car that looked a little suspicious. We quickly headed south by Bill Yerky's. As we rounded the corner, Otto jumped out with the gun and the light. About a quarter of a mile later, a game warden stopped Bill and I. He searched us and the car, and he couldn't find anything, so he let us go. Later, we went back and got Otto and we had a lot of laughs about it. Otto liked to drink. One time, I went over to their house in Kennan, and there was was a Christmas tree with a rope from the ceiling holding it up. Otto said, "I couldn't get it to stand up, so I hung it up." When we wanted to take Bill's sister, Anna Mae along with us, we had to go in and ask him. Does anyone do that today?

My mother was afraid of spiders. One day going to Kennan, up by Jesse Winters' place, Garey and I were in the front seat, and Mom was in the back. This car had doors in the back that opened backwards, and we had a big rubber spider in the back to scare the girls. Well, Mother saw the size of that spider, opened the door and started to jump out. She opened the door and pulled me right off the road, and I stopped real quick. She was so scared that we had to show her that it was just a rubber spider. She said, "You leave that thing right here!" So out in the woods he went. I wonder if any body ever found it.

Dad wanted the fence around the eighty acres checked and fixed one spring, so he offered me and my brother a pair of new Nobbie tires. They were something. Those tires were really good. They cost about twelve dollars for a pair. So we agreed. We started out with a hammer, staples, and of course, our BB guns. It went good for about twenty minutes, then a dumb chipmunk thought he could challenge our marksmanship. Off we went.

About an hour later, back we came and started again. Word must've gotten out about our marksmanship, because there went a squirrel. We had to get him for sure. One hour later, no luck. Back to work. We looked, and it was almost noon! So home we went for dinner. After dinner, we had to walk as far as you could get and still be on our own land, then those squirrels and chipmunks bothered us all day. About 4:00, we had to hurry, because Dad came back at 5:00. We made it just in time. He said, "Boy, you guys sure must've worked if you're done by now." He gave us the money right there. We didn't have the heart to tell him we had done all the work in just two hours. The rest was hunting time. I don't know what it was, but it seemed like we had cows out all summer long that year.

My mother had a nice pearl-handled 22 Saturday Night pistol. We thought she never shot it, so we should try it. We shot it out behind the house when they were milking. They never heard it. Then one day I stuck it in my pocket, and we stopped to climb the straw stack and slide down. The second slide, I said, "Uh Oh!" I lost the gun. We looked for days and never found it. About a year later, Mother asked us if we had seen it, and we said, "Not lately." No one ever told.

Bernice married a Norwegian. Dad always said Norwegians were a cross between a skunk and a rubber boot. He was just kidding, he always liked him. His name was Orland Lawrence Peterson. So we called him Pete.

The first week of high school in Phillips, I told myself, one week and I'm done." But then, as I said, a girl called me Larry, and right then I wished I could go twenty years to school. I couldn't get there soon enough and then hurried home and back up there for a ball game or a show.

My mother did most of the janitor work at the Four Corners school. I just collected the money. I was no angel in school really. I think it was the people I hung around with, like Louis Banyai, Lyle Tews, and Laddie Zellinger. One time, Louis and I used Lyle as a battering ram and broke the lock on the Spanish door. We didn't show up first for class that day. About that time, Mother (I think she knew more than what she told us.) said, "Let's stop at the jail, I'll show you how it works."

We went in and the sheriff, Mr. Pilch took us around, and showed us the inside of a cell, then slammed the door shut. I never forgot that sound, and I never spent any time in jail. I guess my brother didn't learn as fast, because I heard he spent a night in jail, not that he shouldn't have.

One summer day, before I started my senior year, me, Chuck Perdum, and George Winters thought we should go out west and make some money. I knew Mother and Dad wouldn't let me go, so I hid my suitcase outside. We brought Garey home, I grabbed my suitcase, and we were off. With my car. Only one kid had a driver's license, and it wasn't me. We got up to Duluth, Minnesota, and stopped and looked back on the town, it was so nice. About 2:00 in the morning, we stopped to see the Blue ox and Paul Bunyan in Bemidji, Minnesota. Then we got out to Rugby, North Dakota where Chuck had worked last year.

I remember sitting in a cafe in town wondering what to do next. We counted our money. I had twenty dollars, and they each had two dollars apiece. We were a long ways from home, so we went job hunting. We went to the

Bell ranch where we got a good meal, but no work. We checked out a couple of other places, but no work. So I said, "Let's head for St. Paul." We got there early and had some fried eggs. Then I saw the bus guys with lunch boxes getting on the buses. I said, "This isn't for me." But, in 1955, I was back in St. Paul doing that very same thing. Anyways, I said, "Let's go home." I was homesick. So we headed for home. After I took Chuck and George home, I went home too, and Mom gave me the biggest piece of pie I ever had, and it never tasted better. I had been gone a week, and when Dad came home from work, I thought, "Boy, will I hear it now." So me, always saying something smart, said, "Hello, see ya got the same dog yet." He laughed. I was happy to be home, and they were glad I was back. I still get homesick, and nothing will ever help until I get home. I'm not a good traveler. The sad part of the story is, two days later, we went into Schancer's store to get chicken feed. Mrs. Schancer said, "Did you hear about George Winters?" I said, "No." She said, "He drowned last night in Hanson's swimming hole." I often wondered, if we had found work, would he be alive today? If I hadn't got homesick? Maybe. Who knows.

I went to school in Phillips from 1950 to 1951, we had a small bus, and it wasn't yellow. All the buses were red, white, and blue. Our bus driver was Herman Seeger. He would watch us in the mirror. Heaven knows why. We would always sing Beautiful Brown Eyes to him. The poor man sure earned his pay. One time, the little bus broke down on 111 about a mile from Highway 13. Herman walked to make a phone call to the school to get help. While he was gone, some hoodlums got out of the bus and threw stones at it, and broke the radiator, some seats, and other things. When

Herman and the new bus came back, they were furious. They took us back to school and questioned each one of us. I must've blacked out, because I didn't recall seeing anything, or maybe I was reading a book. Anyways, only Louis Banyai said, "I did some of the damage." I always thought that took a lot more guts than blacking out or reading a book.

My teen years would not be complete without telling about the time I got shot. Bill Schoenfelder and I went hunting by the train bridge in Catawba. Bill had a long Tom gun. Up went a partridge. BANG! He shot and I was flat on my back on the ground. One BB from the shot had hit me right above the eye. Oh, it hurt. I thought my days were over, but it wasn't too bad. I went home and asked Mother to look at it. She said, "Just a bruise, no hole." Hallelujah!

I graduated in June 1952 in a class of sixty-seven. I think I should have been ranked number eighty in our class, because I wasted a lot of time. I learned a lot, but I sure wasted a lot. The teacher I remember most is Mr. Ed Falstad. The first day, he said, "They call me Cold-Hearted Ed. You'll find out why."

Personally, I did. We had to write a paper about something for History class. As I was too busy to waste my time on thinking, I went to the library and copied it from a book. Word for word. The next day, he asked me to read it, and I did. He said, "Larry, I can't believe you're so smart. Why, that's the very same thing the Encyclopedia has in it!" If there would have been a hole small enough for me, I would've crawled in it. After that, I had to make it up, so I really did study History, and now I love it. He's still alive in Ladysmith, and someday, I'll tell him that if it wasn't for that copying deal, I wouldn't have loved History, or wrote this book. I knew I was on the bottom end of our class, but one guy beat me. Dean Haffa. He had one credit, and he went to the last day of school. But life was good to him. He got a job with Caterpillar repair, and traveled all over and made good money. He just didn't get school.

Most of our class did real well. Just to mention a few, Del Worsech was a lieutenant colonel in the air force. Bill Baratka was part owner of Phillips Plating, and Ron Helland, who was a state trooper. We had lots of schoolteachers, and I don't know one that got in trouble or was a bad person.

I know Laddie Zellinger would not think my story was complete without the story of the free shot. It was a ball game. Last second. I was at center court. I took a hook shot, and the buzzer rang. We won by one point. As years go by, and the story is retold, it was a conference basket ball championship game and we won the title with that shot. And no one, and I mean no one was more surprised than me.

Let's talk about Halloween when I was young. Oh yes, we did a little mischief. One time we went up to a place on J that we thought might need a little adjustment, so my brother Garey and Jack Hvass headed for the outhouse while I drove Garey's old '28 Chevrolet. But, they were waiting, and the boys came running back for a quick getaway. What? In a 1928 Chevrolet? No way! They knew who we were and followed us around for a while, and ruined our whole night out. One time, we went and pushed over Greenwall's toilet up on the north road. No one lived there then, but a few years later, I bought that place. I sure could've used it a few times.

Ray Hampton lived across the road from us. On this Halloween, Ray sat in the dark and waited. About 8:00, my dad walked over and said, "How's it going Ray?" He said, "Everything's okay on the western front." Dad said, "Oh, Ray, what's that wheelbarrow doing on your roof?" He jumped in his big Buick and drove all over, but didn't see a thing. The big boys also tipped over the Four Corners' outhouse and the first people they blamed it on were the Pfaffendorf boys. But we had alibis, and later they found the real crooks. In Hawkins, they put the principal, Mr. Deturk's Volkswagon up on the school roof. On Monday, he called all the kids to the gym, and he said, "Do you think you're funny?" He never found out who it was. No you're wrong, it wasn't us.

I should mention that with our car we got around. We went to Hawkins chasing girls, and the boys over there didn't like that at all. I remember Jerry Martinson took my new spinner for the steering wheel. He grabbed it, threw it on the blacktop and broke it.

My dad had arthritis so bad he couldn't even comb his hair. What little hair he did have. So he would take a honey bee out of the hive, put it on his arm and make it sting him. I don't know if it worked or not, but even after he turned ninety, he still moved like a fifty year old, and no arthritis.

Garey and I would take a car and go over to Harvey Hvass' place and play ball. Garey and Jack would be one team, and I got Judy and their little brother Buddy. I don't think we ever won a game. That's the way Garey and Jack had it figured. One time I was mad over losing again and I told Garey he could walk home. And he did. Poor loser wasn't I?

We also had 4-H meetings at night, so Garey and I would take our Schwinn bikes in the summer evenings. Mostly, we had these meetings at Clifford Hvass' place. We learned a lot from those meetings, and then we played hide-and-seek after dark. Then we headed for home with our little bike lights on. If you hit a bump, out went the light. I wonder how many deer and bear got scared by that crazy bunch. How we made it, I will never know.

As a young man out of high school, I got a job with a farmer. Not too bad either. Thirty dollars a month, room and board. I didn't last too long there. They thought I should hoe potatoes after supper, and I had so many other things to do. That was my first job away from home. Then I hauled lime for George Mustard. He drove one truck, and Louis Banyai and I shoveled the lime in by hand in the other truck.

Then I was going with a girl from Kennan, and she was a friend of Carol Haskins. They invited us down to play ball. I loved to play ball. So we chose sides and started to play in cow pie stadium in Pennington. I always batted over third base, but that day, I batted to first base. Every time I was up, the girl on first put me out. I sure didn't go for that. After the game, we all went down to the Haskins' home and had supper. Mrs. Haskins had fried potatoes and were they good. Then I found out that first baseman was Elaine Haskins. We kinda hung around until after dark, and I asked her for a date for Saturday. She said, "Sure." So I was all set. As she got ready for Saturday night, her dad said, "Forget it, he's got a girlfriend already." But soon I came, and we went to the movies. On the way home, I felt sick, so I dropped her off, and by the time got home, it was worse. I woke up my brother Garey and Mother, and said, "I have to go to the hospital. I think I have appendicitis." On the first date. They did surgery the next morning.

Elaine had left to go to camp to work in Lac Du Flambeau. About a week later, I got home. Then I got her address and started writing. Soon we were going steady. We had a lot of fun, and also a lot of arguments. Later, I decided to join the army. We were supposed to get married New Year's Eve, and I found out they wouldn't take me in the army if I was

Lawrence [Larry] William Pfaffendorf

Elaine Mae Haskins

Married June 4, 1955.

married. So I went to Minneapolis for a physical. I was so lonesome. I thought, "This is not for me." And as luck would have it, they only took two men out of a hundred and thirty-five. That was right after the Korean war. They were downsizing. Of course, I talked my friend Louis Banyai into enlisting. He went the next week, and he was history. That's the way it goes. So not getting into the army, I didn't have a job or money. Elaine's dad and brothers, Bob and Don, were looking for work also. So Grandpa Lee, as we called Elaine's dad, said, "Let's go to Ely and work in the woods." So we went up there, and couldn't find work. My dad was working in a saw mill at Forest Center, Minnesota. He went up there at age sixty-five to build up his social security. We thought about it, and went back to the Forest Center and got jobs in the woods. The first night, we stayed at camp two. They had a big bunk house, and we slept there. In the morning, it was thirty below zero and Don's car wouldn't start. So we took the oil out and heated it up, and the old Oldsmobile started. So then we went up close to the Canadian border, only fifteen miles away, to a camp called Private Lake. This camp was sixty-five miles from town. If you got hurt real bad, you could just kiss it goodbye. The boss took us out to look over the timber. It was bad, but we decided to stay. They gave us two horses. Don and Grandpa Lee had Moose, Bob and I had Joker. Joker would run back to the barn every chance he got. Don had an old McCulloch chainsaw, and Bob had a one-handled Titian. I was the teamster for me and Bob. I always rode the horses out and back at night. Now, to be a teamster, you had to be 1/4 mouth, and 3/4 crazy to do it. I also fed and watered the horses while the others cooked. We had a hole for drinking water. There was one for the horses too. In the spring, after break up, we saw it was just a swamp. We lived in a tar paper shack with an air tight stove. It was either too hot or too cold. No in between.

We had about twenty shacks in our camp, and the toilet was on the opposite end of camp. One time, Grandpa Lee put too much soap in the dish water, and we all got the diarrhea. We couldn't make it to the toilet on the other side, so we just headed across the road. One would come back across the road, and hand the paper to the next one. Really nice fishing up there. No one but us could go in there. And the beavers. They were big and old because no one trapped them. There were also a lot of moose tracks, and sometimes at night, as you laid there in your bunk, you could hear Timber wolves howl. Boy, the hair on the back of your neck would stand straight up. The air was so still, you could hear for miles. One time, as we laid in our bunks, almost asleep from our long day out in the woods, we heard music coming from somewhere. Good accordion music. In a little bit, there came a bunch of lumberjacks that had been to Ely and had gotten drunk, and ran their car into the ditch. They were walking home to the next camp. It sure sounded pretty, way up there in the timber.

We didn't make much money, but we ate well and felt good out in the cold air and hard work. One night, a guy knocked on our door. He had been in the hospital and had gotten a ride to our camp. He wanted us to give him a ride to his camp a ways down the road. Well, let me set the scene, we didn't know this guy and it was dark. We drove him home, and we had to go in to see his partner. His partner was something else. Only a dim lantern for a light. He got out all his detective books, and told us about all the murders around the country, and all the gruesome details. I always thought he was old Ed Gein, who was a guy from Wisconsin who dug up people's graves and killed and ate people.

Other times, we would come home for the weekend. We had to go through a toll booth in Duluth, and Grandpa Lee said, "Cover me up and see if we can get through." So we pulled up to the toll bridge and the guy on duty said, "You wanna pay for the guy in the backseat?" We had a good laugh about that. Grandpa Lee took us down to skid row one time, in Duluth. Hobo capital of the world. That was scary. Some real weird guys around there!

Lawrence Pfaffendorf

One time, Grandpa Lee and Don were going back to Ely. They had a watermelon and some tomatoes in the back seat. The watermelon rolled back and forth all the way up to Ely, and when they got there, all they had left was tomato juice.

Oh yes, we drank a little too. One time, it was Ten High. We had a lot of that, and on the way home back to camp, Bob was driving and hit a snowbank. Then Don drove home. We got to our shack and thought it would be nice to put up an aerial in a tree. We could get better reception. So Bob, who was afraid of heights, goes up in a tall white Birch, and says, "Here's where we should have it." Then I climbed up and put it up. He could've done that all in one trip. I needed to walk to the toilet on the other side of camp, so I walked real slow so no one would know I was drunk, because I was a little wobbly.

The next spring, we thought we would try a different company called Northwestern. Only me, Don, and Lee stayed. Bob had went home to work for the Rusk county highway department. We had two shacks and an old gravel pit. Talk about hot! When the sun hit it, that was really great. That was where we met Chuck Hall. Grandpa Lee took him home, and his daughter Doris Haskins ended up marrying him later. In May, I wrote a letter and told Elaine, "Lets get married in June." Well she never got the letter, and when I came home in June, she was really surprised. But, we thought we could do anything, so we decided that June 4, 1955 would be the day we got married. We were married in Kennan at the Lutheran Parsonage by Reverend Wudel. Howard and Doris Haskins stood up for us. Then we went to Prentice, and almost had a bad car accident in Catawba. We got to our small reception and got some gifts and a little money. At about 3:00, we were going to head for Ely. Just as we left, Arnold, Elaine's uncle, gave us twenty bucks. And we were off. We made it to Superior that night and spent our honeymoon there. The next day, on to Ely. We got back to camp, and Grandpa Lee said, "The boss said, 'No more job.'." We had only twenty dollars left. He said they had found some trees I hadn't trimmed out. I don't know about that. But he said, "I'll check with the boss to see if he'll keep you on." So he did and we stayed. That was our first home. A tar paper shack fifty miles from town. One room 10 x 12 and a 3/4 bed. Heck, we just snuggled up, and we had lots of room. Two nights later, the camp shiveried us. There were two other couples. An Indian couple, I never knew their names, and a Cornwell girl and her new husband. So we went to Ely and got some beer. Our share was twenty dollars, so we were flat broke until payday. But that was one month away, so we charged food at the store and made it. Come payday, we got a check for seventy-five dollars after our food was paid.

We were going home that weekend, and we said, "We can't live on this." So at home Elaine went back to Lac Du Flambeau, and I got a job driving milk for Ray Schwartz at five dollars a day. Most of the time, there were no brakes on the truck. Some close calls. One time, I hit Mrs. George Mustard as I turned into Ted Kirmse's. She didn't get hurt, thank goodness. This was all cans and they were heavy. One time, I was supposed to grease the truck, and I missed the universal joint. Don Lebal was driver and he bawled me out. I never forgot that. Next time I was more careful. That went until fall. Don Haskins came home and Chuck Hall and I went to St. Paul to look for a job. I got a job working at a box factory called Weinhagens on 8th street. Don and Chuck didn't find work. My brother Garey and Jack Hvass were there about a month, so I said, "I'll stay with them and try it." They had an apartment on Summit Avenue. A nice walk. So I worked there a little while and Jack went home, so I said, "I'll bring my wife here." Garey, Elaine, and I lived there, and as soon as Elaine came, we found out we were expecting. Things were really moving fast. When she was about seven months along she got sick, so we called the doctor. He looked at her and said how much the call would cost. That was about all the money we had put away. We squirreled away a little money every week. We hid it in a ceiling light in an old matchbox. It was just enough to cover the bill. Broke again. Soon our oldest son was born. We named him Lonnie, after a singer we liked. His middle name was Larry. Elaine was in the delivery room, and the nurse came out and said, "You have a son." I said, "Thank you." One other guy said, "You don't have to thank them, they're just doing their job. When Lonnie was born, he had hair all over. I said, "Let's take him out to Monkey Island in Como Park. That's where he belongs." He had some problems as a baby. He couldn't nurse because mother's milk just didn't agree with him, so we put him on the bottle. We were poor and didn't have a proper crib for him or anything. The crib he had was what they called a Layette. It was made like a chest. By this time, Garey had moved out by cousin Melvin in Wyoming, Minnesota.

I also worked nights for a security company. Checking buildings, and working with the St. Paul police. On occasions, I thought I might like to be a cop, but I changed my mind after I saw what they had to see and do.

Elaine's sister Carol came and helped out during the summer and we made it. Elaine got a job and that helped too. I got a better job at Waldorf paper company out on University Avenue. My sister Bernice had Lonnie for a while too. We were expecting again. This one we had planned to name Scottie Trace. So, Elaine went home to my mother, and my dad was still up in Ely. We were in for a big surprise.

One day, I took Elaine up to Lapham's Maternity home in Phillips. Things were okay, so I went home. I called in the morning to see how everything was. Mrs. Lapham said, "You have two boys." I said, "Oh boy!" As I had to go back to St. Paul Monday, and since Elaine's brother lived in Prentice, I asked him to pick her up. We didn't have any names picked out for the twins, so Elaine's sister Carol said, "Timmie and Tommie." We never thought, or we would have named them Tim and Tom. When my dad came home from Ely the next weekend, he said, "If they make it through the winter, they might make it." We kept them in back of the oil stove in the old house. During this time, I had moved from Summit to Igehart. Garey and Joe Kostis lived with me. Elaine was here also until she went home. It was lonesome in St. Paul while my wife and three boys were in Kennan.

We had some money and we bought some land north of the homeplace in Georgetown. The Greenwalt place. We thought about living there, but there was no house or anything. Soon I quit in St. Paul and came home. In the spring, Dad quit in Ely and Mother and him moved to St. Paul with Garey. We made a deal to buy the farm and seven or eight cows. We thought we had it made. Wonderful. It wasn't long and the bills were bigger than the income. Our fourth child was born. Sherrie. Named after Sherrie Crane, Rita Hayword's daughter. Now four kids on a small income. My mother said, "Don't you think that's plenty?" I guess she was right, and we didn't have anymore for a while. I went to work in the woods with Don up to Boulder Junction the summer Sherrie was born. We made good money. We worked two weeks in a row and each made $300. We moved to Trout Lake next. There was a game warden that had a garden in the back in the woods, of course, the guys found it. There was a fence around it, but they got in anyway, and took his tomatoes and other stuff. Boy, he was hot! If he would've found out who it was, they would've been down the road. We all knew, but no one had told. Chuck and Doris were there at this time. Don and I then moved to Lemington, Wisconsin and had a hard winter. There Don got hit in the nose with a spring pole and I got a dislocated little finger. Come spring, I put in for a job at Norco Windows in Hawkins. They wouldn't hire me because I was out of town. That fall, I went back and asked again. They said, "I'll let you know."

Uncle Pete, Bernice's husband, was working there then, and they were hiring more people. I went to see my mom and dad in Minnesota. I got a call the next day to report to work, so back I came.

Pamela Dawn was born on Christmas day. Our fifth and last child. She was the one for old age and it had worked out that way. She takes good care of us, and is always calling to check up on us. We named her Pamela because we liked that name. The middle name Dawn came from Mrs. Paul Gehring's sister. I was at Paul

Gehring's wedding and I thought it was such a nice name.

The factory was better than the woods. Don and I had worked down by Broken Arrow in Ladysmith, and I drove every day. So this was a lot better closer to home. I stayed at Norco for thirty-five years and could write a book about that place. I was Union president, foreman, fired once for doing Union work on company time, which I didn't do, but we got the National Labor Relations Board on our case and they had to take us back. Elaine was also there and got fired along with Carol

Cornell and Louis Rudnick. I hadn't known those people, but I soon got to know them as we fought for our jobs. Elaine and I decided to stay there, but the other two chose not to. I always had a good job. I finished up as quality control inspector, the only one in the whole plant. When I was hired, I was the sixty-ninth person there, and when I left, there was over four hundred people working there. We also went on strike three times at Norco. We had to picket four hours every day.

Pam remembered walking with Anne Romanyshank, and she showed Pam where the "green men" on the moon were. One night, when I was sleeping, and Elaine was working nights at Norco, and Pam was seven or eight, she came running into my room and said, "There's a flying saucer on the lawn!" I said, "Get back to bed or I'll break your legs."

Pam cut her little toe on the sink one night when she was little and helping with the dishes. She was crying and it looked bad, so I wrapped it up and told her that we had to go to the doctor. She didn't want to go, but I said, "You have no choice." So in the car we went. The three boys stayed with Auntie and Uncle

Pete while Me, Pam, and Sherrie went to Ladysmith. The doctor said, "Your dad did a good job of wrapping it up." In a little while, she was okay. Another time, when we had a babysitter, Tom cut his foot real bad. Auntie Bernice came down and took him to the doctor.

One time, four of the kids ran away from home. All except Tom. The thought of pulling weeds in the garden was not their thing. They were going to Grandma and Grandpa Pfaffendorf's in Minnesota about 120 miles away. They took the dog with and they had to carry him. I followed so no one would get hurt.

Pam made it about a mile. Sherrie went to the county line, and Tim to Hawkins. Lonnie made it to Hilltop, about ten miles away. When they got home, I said, "If you like to run, run around the house a little while, it's better than running away."

There was a time Tim and Tom were in trouble in the house, so I told them, "You guys can sleep in the barn if you're going to act like animals." They did, and I checked on them before I went to work, and there they were all covered up with a blue tarp. I felt so bad for being so mean to them, and I haven't forgotten it.

Lonnie seemed to be in trouble most of all. He got mixed up with his friends and helped steal some pop from the tavern down the road. One time, I didn't take him fishing, so he started a brush fire by the barn, and then ran to the neighbors. You should have seen his car. The gas tank was a five gallon can in the back seat. He also had two car accidents in one day, and they canceled us out. Now you try to get insurance with three teenage boys and two accidents in one day.

One time, the three boys and the Arquette boys were going to stay up at the cabin and boil maple syrup. Now I find out that they were up in Phillips drunk and they had to push the car to get it started. I had a way to take care of things like that. It was called Kangaroo court. Everybody had their say, and then everyone helped sentence the offender. Of course, I helped a lot.

We had a hole in the porch right by our bedroom for the cat to come in for food. There was a lot of noise out there one night, so I took a broom, and without my glasses, went to see what was going on. I saw the cat and took a swipe at it. The darn thing looked like it humped up, and I said, "You think you're so cocky." Then I took a good swing, and then I knew that it was no cat, it was a skunk, and boy, did the house smell.

I used to outlaw at night so we had meat for the family. It was hard times. One time, I went up to the old house on the place where Don Hahn lives now. It was our land then. As there were no steps in the old house, to get upstairs, you had to grab the sides and pull yourself up.

That night, being warm and humid, the whole floor was full of pine snakes. All sizes. I've never seen so many, and I don't want to ever again. There was also an old rock well there which was also a wonderful place for snakes. Garey and Jack Hvass always liked to shoot them. One day, they had a bright idea. They got a bale of hay, poured gasoline on it, threw it in the well then started it on fire. When that got hot, there were snakes coming up all over. You should've seen those boys run to the car.

As long as we're on the topic of hunting, one moonlit night, I was out outlawing on the

Johnson place where Logan Edinger lives now. I was sneaking down the road and it was a real quiet night. All of a sudden, a screech owl hollers. Was I scared. No more hunting that night. We only had two gun accidents when we were young men. One time, I had Dad's old 12 gauge shot gun loaded, bouncing up and down on my big toe with the barrel down on my toe. I moved it over to the floor and BANG! A hole in the kitchen floor. The other time, Garey was showing Elaine his new unloaded 22 rifle in the house. BANG! A hole in the ceiling. It could've killed her. When we got low on meat, me and two other guys would go shining. One guy was a good shot at night. I would drive and the other would jump out and gut the deer. We took a lot to feed our families, but we never wasted it.

For a while, we got interested in Stock cars. Me and Elaine's brother Norm bought one. Norm would drive it in the Phillips races. Never won much. We also made a race track up on Greenwall's and had a lot of fun with it.

I guess I better tell you about one horse buying trip. That was pretty rough. Me, Don, and Norm went up to Park Falls to see Monte

Passer about buying a horse. He also owned a tavern. He wasn't home, so we waited for him. We drank some beer, played some pool, and drank some more beer. We thought we better head for home. Don driving, me in the backseat, and Norm in the passenger seat. We got on 111 and Norm had to go for a "walk". I guess it was real slippery, because he fell on his back and looked like a whale spouting. We got home, and Don had to take Norm in the house, and then came to get me. We both had to go to bed. I stayed in bed for three days. That was the end of my drinking. Never again.

Norm watched basketball and said that he saw two number seventeens with the same ball.

It was a close neighborhood when we all first got married, then sadness hit. George Kostis was putting up hay, and his little girl ran behind the tractor and was killed. All the neighbors got together and hauled hay for him on a field way up on Heacock's hill about 4 miles away. Elaine's brother Gene was with us then. Just a kid. I had a John Deere A tractor and I was hauling the loads down to George's place. There was another neighbor, Fritz Lebal. He had a little Farmall tractor. We passed him three times before he got one load home. He just sat there smoking his pipe and putting along. Almost all the old neighbors are gone or moved away. Me, Bob Kirmse, Emma Arndt, and Ralph Lebal are the only four left.

There was a time, when there was an ad in the paper. They wanted people to go to school to learn how to take care of their forests at home. So I joined up. It was the first covet program and is still going today. We went out to Kraft Paper Company's old homestead in Woodruff. They used this for school, and we studied all day. At night we had a steak feed cook out. then as night came, we all laid down in our sleeping bags in rows. About eight people per row. This place had no electric, so we had a few flashlights and everything went good until about two o'clock. Then a weasel came out, unknown to us, to look for his supper. For some reason, the weasel jumped on the first man's face, he jumped of course, and the weasel takes off across the faces of all the other men. The last man in the row, a quiet older guy, said, "Boy, he sure had cold feet didn't he?" We laughed about that most of the night.

A thing our little family did was, every Friday, we would go get hamburgers and french fries from the Long Branch bar. Gerald and Edna Moore ran it at that time. Boy, they sure tasted good. Edna was such a good cook. I can still smell it!

When I was middle-aged, I took a trip to Germany to see our oldest son. We had never flown before, and I was scared. I wouldn't look out the window, but when I saw how beautiful the sky and clouds were, they couldn't get me away from it. Of course, the lady by us was from Germany, and made a trip home every year. She had married a G.I. She said, "Don't worry, the pilot wants to get home too." That was a big help. Hadn't she heard of accidents? We made it to England but couldn't land because there was too much fog. So we sat up there and waited. We saw jets come up through the clouds, and I thought, "I hope they know we're up here!" We went on to Germany and landed. The day before, some men were shot on the runway. It was some terrorists. We stayed at our son's house in the army base. We played the slot machines and I hit the jackpot on the nickel ones, so then Lonnie's kids, Jessie and Sonya, helped me spend it until some lady came in and said, "Those kids are too young to play." The fun was over. A couple of days later, we left for Denmark by train. We couldn't speak Danish. When we arrived in Denmark at night, the lady at the hotel could speak English. Thank goodness! We had a good trip, and it was exciting not being able to communicate with anybody. One lady learned English forty years earlier and she was able to say things to us. We came home in a snow storm and were happy to be home.

I worked most of my adult years for Northern Sash and Door, now Norco Windows, in Hawkins. Many interesting days there. I worked there for thirty-five years. Our family grew up and left home. The old empty nest syndrome. It sure was nice for a while, but then I got lonesome for them. They would all come home for Christmas, and sometimes weekends. Lonnie joined the Army out of high school. He spent eighteen years in there. He also married Cheryl Wettstein. She had a son from a previous marriage named Jesse. Lon and Cheryl had a daughter, Sonya. They later divorced. Tim worked one summer at Norco, then went to Eau Claire to become a hairdresser. He worked in Eau Claire for a while, then he went to Green Bay to the mall.

Later, he owned and operated his own salon. He met and married Cathy Schmidt. They had a son named Kyle. They built several homes, and now live in the last one he built. Tom also works at Norco Windows. He met and married Naomi Severson. They have two children, Megan and Matt. Tom and Naomi went to LaCrosse, where she went for nurses' training. Tom also worked there at a sports shop. But they came back, and Tom works at Norco and they live by Hawkins on their little farm. Sherrie married John Terry, and they had one son, Neil. He was my helper for a long time. He now works at Norco, and has gone into fire-fighting and ambulance service. He helps a lot of people and we are very proud of him. Sherrie and John divorced. Then she married Mike Nikkila. They lived in Prentice and had no children. They also divorced. She then married Matt Miller and they had three children, Samantha, Victoria, and little Matt. They lived in Ogema and lost their home to a fire. They bought another home on Fairview road. They sold that and then they bought land from us and built a new home. Lost that to a fire. They rebuilt a very nice home. Then Sherrie started to work at Norco. Then her and Matt divorced. She later married Ricky

Johnson. He had a daughter from a previous marriage named Alysha. Pam didn't get married yet. She has four children. Katelyn Arquette, who helped me on this book. She is a great artist. Then the twins, Mitchell and Luke Haugsby. Then little Katrina Haugsby. She used to be Grandpa's girl, but now she is growing up and she just teases Grandpa. So we have twelve grandchildren plus a step-grandchild. No one married yet. But, when they do, I suppose I'll have to write another book. I think I enjoyed the older adult years most of all. The children and grandchildren

My Family

back row: Tom, Tim

2nd row: Elaine, Larry, Lonnie

front row: Pamela, Sheryl

were always around. Now only Pam and her kids come, and Neil when he can.

We had raised registered shorthorn beef cattle for some years, but we sold them all about the time the kids left home, and started planting Christmas trees for retirement. Every fall, we used to cut Balsam boughs on the land that we had owned in Pennington. We started out at nine cents a pound. Now, it's almost thirty cents a pound. We could cut ten tons most years. One year, I cut my leg with a saw, and I had to go to Medford to get it all sewed up. I always told everyone that I just threw my leg over my shoulder and headed for the road, almost a mile away. Of course, that's not true. I just wrapped it with my red handkerchief, and it didn't bleed too bad. Our grandson Neil also helped us cut down home. Now we cut a little bit on our Christmas tree plantation. Our farm was 240 acres with woods and a little cleared land. The home eighty has five acres under plow. The rest is Christmas trees and hardwood forest. The eighty acres north of the homeplace, where Don Hahn now lives, was almost twelve acres under plow. We sold that to him, and he has a nice new home there. Our other eighty acres was our first piece of land we bought. Greenwall's place. On the corner of Fairview and Oak ridge, about a mile north of the homeplace. We sold that also, and Ron Runnheim's family lives on it today. They have now subdivided it and their two children each have a part. The girl, Veronica, got married to Trent Tobias, and they are building a new house there. Forty acres of this place was once owned by my uncle John Thompson. We also owned a hundred acres in Pennington. Also now sold. In 1990, we bought the Tulpan place to the west of us. We also got Lottie and Ed Lebal's place. All part of Mrs. Lebal's father, Herman Fritz's land. Mr. Herman Fritz and Mrs. Ernest Rothe came from Germany. Mr. Rothe lived here on our place. Herman Fritz lived on the next place west. Herman had a wife and a daughter Lottie. Ernest was a bachelor. They built houses just alike, about 1902. They were the head carpenters when they built the Four Corners school in 1902. Rumor was, they took all the good lumber for their houses, and gave all the poor lumber to the school house. Ernest had donated one acre of land to the school. The school and Herman Fritz's house still stand. Joe Marshall's family now lives in it. We tore ours down, and built a new house where the old barn was. The old house was home to Ernest Rothe, then the McQuay family lived there. It was also home to some old people. It is said that Jim Knight died there and was laid out for viewing in the living room. Uncle Andrew Thompson bought it about 1946. Then he died, and my mother and father bought out uncle John Thompson, and we moved here that year. Highway 8 was being paved about 1947. Elaine and I bought it in the 1960's.

One time, we came down here to help Uncle Andrew shingle the house. Garey helped a little. At dinner, we had a big bologna.

Garey's eyes were always bigger than his stomach and he ate half a ring all by himself. He said, "Don't tell Mother how much I ate." That's more or less the history of our farm.

During my later adult years, I worked at Norco. First, I took away from two cutoff saws by Adam Gryga and Ed Tomaszewski. Ed always was hollering. I thought he was mad at me. Adam said, "No, that's just Eddy!" Later we became very good friends. Then one day, my foreman, George Odelle said, "Can you drive a tractor?" I said, "Sure." He said, "Go run the big fork lift in the lumber shed and bring up some lumber to the cutters." So I did, and I stayed out there for a couple years. Then I put in a job working nights. There was better pay, and I needed the money. It only lasted a year or so, then I went on the cut off saws on days. About this time, the place burned down of unknown causes. the union workers worked two weeks with out pay, and we lost lots of fringe benefits. Bill Best was the president of the union for a while. He had a good way of doing things. I became a strong union man. Bill got a job in the office that didn't last long. After some time, Norman Haskins, my brother in law, became president and we had a strike.

No one knew what to do, so Joe Babulla said, "Give me a sign." He was our first picketer. Norman got hurt in a snowmobile accident and had a rough time for a few years. I was vice president, so I became president. I never held a meeting. Warren Holzem asked if I'd like to be supervisor, and in a short time I was a foreman. Then I saw how they worked. You couldn't help your workers. I helped Lloyd Slack with some problems he had with insurance. He didn't understand. George Quinn, or Big Daddy, as we called him, said, "Don't do that again." Johnny Gang also worked in my department, and if he got mad at you, John put your name on a cross and put it outside. Soon it looked like a cemetery. He had all the big wheels included. One day, Warren Holzem saw it. Then I was in hot water. I told John to take it down. He did. He was a heck of a good worker, and an all around good guy. I became very disenchanted with the foreman job, as there was no future, all you could do was say, "Yes." So I had some problems with the management and we agreed it was not the job for me. So went back to the stockroom. But I had rejoined the union, good thing. Warren Holzem gave me my check and said, "Don't forget, this is company land and company property." I thought maybe he was firing me because he thought I had stolen something. At quitting time, I found out that my wife Elaine, Carol Cornell, and Louis Rudnick were also fired for doing union business on company time. I didn't even know the other two people. But thank goodness Louis knew more than us. He contacted the National Labor Relations Board, and after a month, we were told that the company had to rehire us. Elaine and I went back to work and nobody ever harrassed us. I went back as a door cut off person and made good bonus there. Then a job as a quality control inspector opened up. A new job. I got it, and at first it was a lot of work. I had a lot of bosses. Bruce Evjen was the one I had the longest. He was a buyer in the office. One time he said, "Larry, you're the most bull headed guy I ever saw." Maybe he was right. In later years, I had helpers that unloaded products and I checked them and rejected what wasn't up to our standards. I also inspected windows and so forth. It was a good job. Charlie Pobanz was my last boss. Him and Rick Hoff. They had an office upstairs. When the new company bought us, Charlie and Rick were let go. I stayed until July 1st, then I retired.

I mentioned the new house we thought we should build. I had remodeled the old house, but we had no inside bathroom, and the upstairs rooms weren't that good. So we applied for a loan in Ladysmith. We had jobs, and the land, so they gave us the loan for twenty years. I thought, "I'll never pay that off!" About halfway through, Elaine got Asthma and was very sick. Many times she thought she would die. She of course didn't. Pam also got sick and had surgery for a growth on her back and side. We had company insurance, but that didn't cover the bills. Soon we were behind on our house payments. They wrote us a letter telling us we had thirty days to pay up the loan or they would foreclose. What were we to do with the family and the sicknesses? I had to humble myself and go see the loan company if there was some chance. I begged and pleaded. The lady said, "If you can get $2500 in here by next Friday, we will keep your loan." That was like telling me to go get a million dollars. Where would I get that? So I took a ride over to see my dad in Minnesota. I told him I needed money or I was going to lose my home. He felt sorry and he went and got the money from his account. I signed a loan paper to pay so much interest per year. That I did, but Dad died before I could pay him back, and Garey got excited about that. Garey and I were close as kids. I once kept him from getting a licking from Dad. One he deserved. He cut the bladder on my basketball and Dad was going to give him a good licking. That would've been the first licking he ever gave to us boys. I stood up for him and said, "I guess you'll have to lick us both." But, he didn't try. Thank goodness. Garey was in a bad car accident in Germany when he was in the Army. He sat in the middle of the car and they hit a bridge head on. The other two were killed. The army and that accident changed him a lot.

I always said my brother Garey died in Germany and they sent some other guy in his place. We never got along, and still don't. He has two girls and a boy. I don't even know them and he doesn't know any of mine except for Lonnie.

My parents were good, hard working people. They didn't seem to have a lot of time for us boys. They were good to us, but no affection. No one ever said, "I love you." or, "You sure are doing great." Mother would tell us stories about our family, which I liked and have worked on family history off and on most of my life. My dad never said anything bad to us or beat us. Nor did Mother. My father's father, Grandpa Pfaffendorf, changed his name when he came to America from Burnhart. The exact spelling is unknown. I have been unable to find anything on it, such as a birth certificate. He said he was a saxon. His name was Herman Henry Pfaffendorf. His father and older brother were killed in war. He had at least two sisters. His mother died at age 102, about 1914. The children thought the nursing home had killed her. They called it giving her the black bottle. Herman went back home in 1914 to settle his mother's estate. The story is,

My dad's family

left to right: My dad William, his mother

Emma, Fred on her lap. Henry, Herman his

dad.

My father's family.

left to right: Henry, Martin, Herman, Mary,

Emma, Ernest, William my dad, Fred.

he ran away from home with his fiance's sister, my grandmother. She was also pregnant. Their son Karl, died soon after birth. He also sold his stepfather's horses to get money to come to America. My grandma was Emma Henrietta Raunberg. She was born or raised across the street from the home of Dr. Martin Luther. She also had some sisters. The sister Herman was supposed to marry did get married, but had no children, and she begged Herman and Emma for one of their children. Each child said it was them who was going to Germany. But, in the end, no one went at all. My dad was in the first World War in Germany and he met what they called their Dutch uncle. How he is related I don't know. His name was Herman Haase. I wrote to him one time and asked him about my grandfather. He said, "I don't know anything about him."

My dad had the vocabulary of a drunken sailor, which he used on the horses. I never heard him swear at Mother or us boys. Of course, he never had reason to. He chewed Copenhagen snuff. That was fifteen cents a box back then. If he ran out, he would walk to the Polish settlement, through the woods, about four miles west. It was five miles to Kennan, so he saved a mile walk. Going both ways, he saved two miles. In those days, that was a long way.

One time, he walked to Kennan to Rudy's service station to get a battery cable. It was dark when he got home and as he came back, he hit the corner of the house with a BANG! We were really scared until Mother said, "It's Dad and one of his jokes." He liked to tell good clean jokes. When John and Marion Hvass came over, and John started to tell stories, we had to go to bed upstairs. But, we would creep down and listen. They sure didn't make any sense to us, but it must've been bad.

Mother was our nurse and caregiver when we were sick. With a cold, she greased us up with Watkin's liniment, and put a wool sock around our neck for a sore throat. We also had a rock hard substance called Alum that she would put in warm water so it melted and then you would drink it. It was so bitter it almost killed you. No vitamin pills. We got cod liver oil every morning. It tasted bad! I can still taste it on a rainy day.

We were born before television, penicillin, Polio shots, plastic, contact lens, and the Pill. We didn't have radar, credit cards or laser beams. Or ball point pens, pantyhose, dishwashers, clothes dryers, electric blankets, or air conditioning. We were born before man walked on the moon. There was no fast food, gay rights, daycare centers, electric typewriter, yogurt, no guys wearing earrings. But, we survived. I grew up in a great time. The Depression was going full force, Hitler was a dictator in Germany, and the Japs bombed Pearl Harbor in 1941. Franklin Roosevelt was our president from 1933 to April 1945. He had

Polio, and some people in our town got it also. Fred Perdum's girlfriend got it too and died about a mile away from our place. Norman Runnheim got it and lived. He was about two miles away. Everyone was afraid. No one knew what it was or how you got it.

One time, when I was in my fifties, our oldest boy Lonnie and his family came to visit. His stepson Jesse was about seven or eight years old, and our little grandaughter Sonya was still in diapers. I told them stories about Captain Kidd, the pirate, and how he used to come up the creek and go into our garden to bury his treasure. I even buried some pennies for them to dig up. Us older people had a good laugh about that. But, when I got up for work about dawn, here were those two kids out there digging for more treasure, and Sonya in her diaper, looking for gold.

One of the neighbors we had in those years was Buster Brown. He always said, "I'm Buster Brown, the homeliest man in town." He had a drinking problem, and sometimes, I had to take him uptown to get some beer. But, I always did, because when I was a little boy, and the American Legion had their Veteran's

Day party, they had Bingo. My dad didn't spend much money on that. It was ten cents a card. Old Buster had a pocket full of dimes and he would give us some to play. I once won a big fish fillet knife. It was the most wonderful thing in the world. So I owed old Buster something for that. He would make bird houses, real nice ones, for days. He also made stocking caps, real nice ones too. Then he'd get that taste for beer, and into town he'd go. He'd sell some of his stocking caps and bird houses and after a while, he'd get too much beer and soon he was giving them away to everyone. He would come home with no groceries, just a bad drunk from all his work. Mrs. Brown sometimes babysat for our kids, and we paid her, but when Buster got thirsty, away went her money. She always said, "My Buster's a good man." And he was, until he got beer.

I retired after thirty-five years of working to feed my family and myself. It's nice to have money coming in. If you're sick or want to stay in bed, that's okay. I've been very active in my hobbies, collecting old canning jars. It's fun to find them at garage sales, auctions, or in old homes. I have a very nice collection, and add to it when I can. As I wrote this book, I found out a lot about myself. Some I didn't like. But that's life. As a teen and young adult, I had a hard time getting along with my dad, now I find that most of the book is about what he said or did. When I look down at my shadow, I see my dad there. I also see that I didn't have the time or the skills to raise five children. If I had to do it over again, and knowing what I know now, I probably wouldn't have raised half of them. It is no fun to be a parent to some of our children. The rewards are poor for all the work and hardships I've went through.

I have done many things in my life that now seem wonderful. I have helped a lot of people with their family histories and other things. I still live on the same farm and sell Christmas trees and firewood. My income is as good as working, and the hours are better.

My family loved my retirement, they said, "Grandpa can babysit!" or, "Grandpa can go there or get that." Everyone else worked, so I was the gopher. But I enjoyed it, especially with our youngest granddaughter Katrina. She thought I was the mom and dad wrapped into one.

For hobbies I of course, have the tree farm, but also collect old canning jars. I have over 2,500 and 600 different kinds. It's fun to find them at different sales. You never know where you'll find them. When you see a jar dated 1856, you know that a lot of history has been seen by that jar. If they could only talk.

We have done some traveling. We have a small motor home. We went up to the U.P to see a niece and an old girlfriend I hadn't seen in over fifty years. 2002 was my fiftieth class reunion. It wasn't too far to travel. Just to

Phillips. Fifty kids came out of sixty-seven, and eight have passed away. Several of the classmates stayed by us and went to the parties with us, including my friend Louis Banyai, from southern Wisconsin, and Eileen Reisner from Ladysmith. We had a great time, and I'm looking forward to 2007.

I have also done some volunteer work. I helped some of the older people that couldn't do work around their home. One Christmas I took my grandson Neil, and we went to help and old man that lived alone. He couldn't talk or hear. Neil said, "Grandpa, that was the best

Christamas ever." I've been very active in S.O.U.L (Save Our Unique Lands), fighting to keep the big power line away from the woods and water. It includes a lot of driving and Sunday meetings. We also have a Kennan-Catawba group.

I have enjoyed my older years, because you can slow down and look at things. You have time to smell the roses. My grandson Neil said, "There's more daylight than there is Grandpa." When my dad was in his nineties, he said, "When you get old, you can try anything, and if you don't make it, everyone says, "He's just an old man, so what." My health has been wonderful from the time I had appendicitis on my first date with my to be wife in 1954 until August 2001, when I was diagnosed with Diabetes. So I changed my eating habits, and I take my pills, and most days are great. It's not the end of the world. Friendship becomes more important to me every year. Every classmate is special. I e-mail a lot of them, they're all great and interesting people.

Being a grandparent is a special job just for old people. My grandkids are all so smart. So much smarter than the kids ever were. You also get to go to Grandparent's day, Christmas plays and church plays. I have twelve grandchildren and one step grandkid. Neil is the oldest and has been a close buddy of mine. We did a lot of rock picking, wood hauling, and talking. Megan is a dark-haired girl. She has some health problems, but she likes to play basketball. Matt. P as we call him, is a special person. He has a wonderful personality. He likes people and he likes to talk. He works summers helping a local carpenter. Katelyn is a beautiful blonde, blue eyed kid. She helped me on this book, and she is a great artist. She will have a good life, her mind is so good. Kyle is in Green Bay, but I don't see him as often as I'd like to. When he was small, we'd go look for bear tracks in the woods. His dad, Tim, never liked the woods. Samantha lives close by, but I don't see her much. She likes basketball and is growing to be quite tall. Victoria, now she is something else. She's a jewel. She can tell stories even she believes, and calls me on the phone when she can. Sonya lives around Green Bay, but she has some problems with herself. Like she said, "Me and Dad live in a make believe world." But, I'm still her number one grandpa. Little Matt is young and quite quiet, but soon he'll be a nice young man. Mitchell, he's fun to be by. He reminds me of Tim. He is very smart and likes to find the answers to everything. Luke, a big lovable guy, is the spitting image of his dad. He also likes to go coffee clutching with his dad too. He loves to keep track of dates and years. Last but far from least is Katrina. Pretty blue eyes and blonde hair with a big smile. She just loves to tease her grandpa. All the time! There are just two boys to pass on the name of Pfaffendorf, Kyle and Matt. Some of my grandkids have a lot of my family genes in them. Life sure has changed a lot, from going to town in horse and buggy to men on the moon, and computers and television. I think we have seen some of the best times. The second World War, Korea, Vietnam, and the economy was really something. Cars cost $400 back then, now over $40,000. Our home cost $13,000, and now would cost over $80,000 to build one like it.

The most important thing in life is your family. Unfortunately, mine is not that close to me. Too many conflicts of personality, and too big of egos. No one seems to know how to say the words, "I'm sorry" and mean it. But, maybe someday. One of the things I would like to pass on to my children and grandchildren, is honor your father and mother. They're not perfect, but they're the only ones you'll ever have.

I hope you enjoyed reading this as much as I did writing it. This is how I want my life remembered and how I remember it, because all of this could only happen once in a lifetime.

About the Author

He was born during the Great Depression and understands what being poor means. He also knows that life can be fun even if it's simple.

He is one of the old timers around here that remembers how it used to be when life went at a slower pace, and your family, friends, and neighbors were important to you. He worked in the great forests of Northern Minnesota. At 68 years, he still goes into the woods almost everyday to enjoy it, and he is thankful for the chance to enjoy nature and be a part of it.

He also writes some about his ancestors and heirs in a fun sort of way to make interesting reading.